GRACE, GUTS And GLORY In AMERICA

STORIES and PSALMS OF A MAN SAVED by GRACE

Edwin A. Hill

iUniverse, Inc.
New York   Bloomington

GRACE, GUTS and GLORY in AMERICA
Stories and Psalms of a Man Saved by Grace

iUniverse books may be ordered through booksellers or by contacting:
iUniverse
1663 Liberty Drive
Bloomington, IN 47403
www.iuniverse.com
1-800-Authors (1-800-288-4677)

ISBN: 978-1-4401-0788-7 (pbk)
ISBN: 978-1-4401-0789-4 (ebk)

Printed in the United States of America
iUniverse rev. date: 1/30/2009

Revised: October 18, 2006

DEDICATION

I dedicate this book to my Mother Frances and my Grandmother before her- Augusta. They have both been lamps unto my feet over the course of my life.

These "Women of God" have stood in the gaps all around me year after year, decade after decade. Their "walk" and example has been music to my ears and the sheet music for my journey through every phase of my life. These women are my heroines. These women are my Angels. These women are my Spiritual role models and songstresses for life. May God continue to bless you both, in life and in heaven.

I also dedicate this book to my Sister Denise: A "songbird" in my life and a saving grace in my battle with cancer. What a caring and loving soul she has been to her nine (9) children, her husband **and me,** as sister and bone marrow donor. May God bless you over and over again as he leads you into the future he has already created for you.

I dedicate this book to my wife Brenda, my sons Garon and Marq, my daughters Edenn and Nicole, my stepsons, Devin and Derek and each of their wives, husbands, daughters and sons, my grandchildren.

I love you all very deeply and I thank you for …"MY PSALMS"…

…the songs that you have placed in my life and heart.

Finally, to my co-workers, friends, extended family and fellow believers

in the faith toward a higher purpose and a more common good. Thank you one and all for your part in my life.

Thank you for sharing your life, time, energy, thoughts and prayers.

Contents

Preface

When his desire, thirst and choice to live collide with the tough realities of the times, he reflects extensively and takes you on a retrospective journey through his life in an effort to find hidden answers he (and many men) needs in order to bring happiness to the future....no matter what the cost. What will happen as he searches for new meanings in life, new understandings of old events, new views on family, relationships, spirituality and more?

Struggle with him as he determines life for himself in an era thirsting for individual freedom and liberty. Explore his innermost feelings and witness his evolution from a kind of street urchin in the inner city to a corporate executive. More importantly, take a walk with him as he struggles with the transition from little boy to young man through an era of social strife, anger and suppression. Hear about the way life, spirit and family sustain and survive over barriers of a special kind.

Find out what our society produces in a man that goes beyond what the eye can see to a deeper place that shapes lives and our futures. Learn from his lessons and allow yourself to be swept away for a moment as he determines how he lived and loved in the process of coming to understand life in his own way in 20th century America... for himself... and for many of us. Hear his trials, his tribulations and his "Songs," along with his successes and his losses as life unfolds for him.

From a backdrop of family history based on a thirst for life and a spiritual foundation pre-destined from GOD.....this is his story, this is his "Song".

Chapter 1

Choosing Life Over Death

Choosing Life Over Death

The spring time always raised my spirits and was something to look forward to for me, the "backyard gardener." It seemed I could always predict when the spring sun would breakthrough to warm the earth and bring life anew to the soil and landscape everywhere. Here on the East Coast, that was surprisingly around early to mid-March. The crocuses and daffodils would spring through the mulched soil and herald the start of growth. So, why was I sitting in the parking lot of Delaware Valley Medical Center surrounded by striped asphalt and concrete? Why was this foreboding fear overtaking my mind? What had happened to my body that I was on my way to x-ray for a full-body bone scan? What would the x-ray reveal? What do we do? How bad is it, could it be? I feel fine. How could this happen? Do the doctors know what they are talking about? Can they be wrong? Maybe the records got mixed up? I feel fine. I've had no problems. Why didn't this surface before? I have annual physicals. They've been okay. I feel fine. Maybe a little cholesterol problem, but we knew that. But… CANCER ??!! Multiple myeloma ??!!

I prayed it's the smoldering/latent version. Maybe it will never fully develop. I prayed the x-ray confirmed smoldering versus fully developed myeloma. So, I went to x-ray. The scan looked relatively normal to my eyes.

The day before, I had a bone marrow aspiration (bone marrow sample drawn and tested) at the University of Pennsylvania for level of myeloma in the marrow and was waiting for results from the doctor or his assistant. While leaving Delaware Valley Medical Center I called for the results. I received a return call in about ten minutes.

The doctor, a graduate fellow, was very apologetic for communicating over the phone but wanted to confirm that the marrow sample revealed about a 30% concentration of myeloma cells in my bone marrow. This affirmed "active" myeloma cancer and a need to determine treatment. What a blow!! It's hard to describe the feelings or the interpretation of those words? What does that really translate to?

Does it mean: ...you are going to die? ...you'll be in pain all your life? ...you'll be fine after treatment? ...you've got another six months or six weeks to live?

"What does it mean? What does it really mean? kept vibrating in my mind.

What will this mean to my family? How can they deal with this? How can I deal with this? What about work? What about our plans, the future, tomorrow, today? Where do I go? Who can I trust? Who cares? What does it matter? Who can I trust? Where will I get help? What do I do?

That day I called my wife (a nurse) and told her that I had just left the medical center for x-rays and was informed that I might have a critical disease that needs further evaluation. Her response was, "but how do you feel?" I told her I felt fine but we needed to look deeper at this problem because it could be life threatening.

I'm not sure she ever really heard me. It felt like she was in denial. I didn't get the caring concern and sympathy I think I expected. I didn't hear her breakdown in pain and tears. I didn't hear her scream an awful "Oh no!" or "Oh my God." All of which I thought I was prepared for. None of which I heard. In reality, I wasn't prepared for it in either case. How could I be prepared? I had never been at this point before, neither had my wife. She was no more prepared to "handle it" than I was. What did "handling it" mean anyway? I had no way of being prepared for it, neither did she.

Only last week Brenda and I had been running and walking two to four miles every other morning. We made it a point to hike and jog in the rough terrain of the Upper Bucks County woods and hills. We were working together at sustaining our picture of health for long-life and fun together. I felt fine, looked pretty good for a guy 46 years old, 190 lbs, and 5'10" inches tall. Brenda and I made it a regular routine on Saturdays to get a good workout on the treadmill followed by a weight lifting routine that always left Brenda's muscles burning. It had been my practice, for the past 12 years, to play rather vigorous 4-0n-4 basketball with the guys at the local YMCA for two-three hours most every Saturday afternoon. Other than the common cold and a broken nose playing basketball I had always felt fine, and never been hospitalized.

So, what was happening to me? How could this be? Why? How did it all come to this?

I began to reflect on my life in retrospect. I began to draw on various phases of my past in order to understand how I got to this point. This was a point of facing life over death. This was a crossroad. I had a choice in it!

I chose to stand and fight...like my ancestors had.

After my diagnosis, my conversations with family revealed that this condition I now faced had it's origin in men in my ancestry. My grandfather whom I never knew was stricken and confined to a wheelchair in the early years of my mother's life.

****

Yes, I was hopeful that it was all a bad dream and I wanted to wake-up and have it all not be true. It took months for me to accept it as true. In accepting it, I had several choices in how to fight this battle. My choices were:

1. Ignore the diagnosis and "go on with my life".

2. Accept the diagnosis and pursue a chemo-therapy treatment regimen for the rest of my life.

3. Accept the diagnosis and pursue an autologous bone marrow transplant

(re-cycling of my own chemo-treated bone marrow and blood cells) along with an aggressive chemotherapy regimen for the rest of my life.

4. Accept the diagnosis and pursue an autologous bone marrow transplant from an "unrelated" bone marrow donor with the same or similar blood type, along with a chemo-therapy treatment regimen as warranted based on higher chances of response/rejection possibilities.

5. Accept the diagnosis and pursue an "allogenaic" bone marrow transplant from a "related" sibling's bone marrow, with the same blood type, along with a chemo-therapy treatment regimen as warranted based on lower risk of rejection possibilities.

My heart and mind pondered the pros and cons of the choices in front of me along with the risk/benefit of each. It was difficult to eliminate the first choice.

It wasn't a bad dream after all. It wasn't going to just disappear.

I had to make a decision.

I had to choose to fight or flee.

I had to see myself in the battle and believe that God would see me through.

Choices #2 and #3 didn't sound or feel like a solution or a cure. The thought of long-term chemotherapy was frightening and left me concerned about "quality of life".

Choice #4 sounded risky considering the unknowns of donors outside of Family, the concern for blood borne disease (AIDS etc.) and it also suggested long-term maintenance and chemotherapy that left me concerned.

Choice #5 was only a "choice" if one of my siblings was a match. This also swung in the balance depending on their willingness to be tested and their willingness to undergo the painful bone marrow "harvesting process".

Again and again and again, "choices" faced every one of my siblings and me. Remarkably, maybe miraculously, every one of them chose to say "yes" to both steps in the process. In my view, even more miraculously, the one match out of the five was my sister Denise. The sister, the daughter, the child my Mother thought for a moment to choose to abort. The sister, the mother of nine, yes nine of her own children, was now a match that could save or bring back to life …another life. My life.

My sister Denise was a gift from God to me long before anyone could have known. She had survived life by our Mother's choices and survived bearing nine children of her own and was now making the "choice" to save my life.

Only God knows what choices will present themselves to all of those touched by her….and by me….in the past, present and future.

Likewise, this experience brought me to reflect on "choices" I had made in my life in the past as well as the present.

Choices, choosing the course, choosing the treatment plan, choosing the Hospital, choosing the timing….? Choosing.

Choosing the fight for life was…all mine. Mine alone.

Mine.

Alone.

How had my parents dealt with the difficult choices in their lives ?

Hadn't my ancestors faced trials and tribulations in their lives?

How had they survived the trials and tribulations they faced both in the South and in the North?

Surely they had fought to hold on to life and all that God promised.

Couldn't I….???

****

They sat or stood there motionless. Each of them reflecting a strength and confidence true to the blood that ran through their veins. The sons of the strongest and most intelligent of those selected for the voyage to this, their new home. Intertwined with the American Indian ancestry, they stood there firm in the resolve that they had earned a right to possess the hundreds of acres they farmed as owners and free men since the Emancipation Proclamation.

Nelson Bliss Sr. loved his sons and raised them to be men; free, strong and responsible with their lives and the land they owned. His wife, their mother, was known as Indian Mary, the daughter of an Indian Chief native to the area now called Indianola, Sunflower County, Mississippi – named after her. Their sons names were Nelson Jr., Walter, Ernest, Turner, and Splender.

Central Mississippi and the early 1900 South was not a place for sons of African slaves and Native Americans to own any property, not to mention hundreds of prime delta acreage. The onslaught of white landowners and government officials was relentless.

Over the years life was tough, but life went on. Man against the soil, man against the elements, sons, side by side. Sons against a society that had shaped their strength and forged their vision of what life could be. Wives, mothers and daughters silently holding it all together, in love and spirituality.

At the age of 44, Nelson Jr. took a wife. A spry little lady of 24, Augusta Harris had visited Indianola from her home 100 miles away. In Starkville, Mississippi, Augusta had been an only child, and excellent student. At age 17, she became a school teacher for many of the sons and daughters of emancipated slaves in the rural Post-Civil War south. A very attractive lady with long black hair surrounding a face with cheekbones that showed her African and Native American heritage. Her mother had been the second wife to George Harris from the Carolina's.

Augusta's mother was a "gift" to the master's residence to care for the plantation owners children.

I began to imagine being with Augusta in her hometown.

She directed the car down a dirt road barely visible through the overgrowth of vines and fern. The oak and walnut trees cling to one another and sway in the wind creating a "windsong" like the Church choir on Sunday morning. The fence posts and stone walks were barely visible through the brush as we walked from the end of the road to the place that marked the front gate.

I could hear her speaking to us as she said….. "This is where we lived, this is sho' noff it. I know because the gate swings in." As we pushed the rust worn gate forward, it creaked and swung true to form as she described the wooded area that bordered what was now open acreage, plowed and furrowed over in ribbons of red clay soil that stretched almost to the horizon to the left as we walked. It was possible, if your mind's eye enabled you, to see where the house would have stood, where the wood pile was, where the "wash pot" boiled the dirty clothes, torn on the briars that radiate from the rugged cotton plants that demanded attention and picking in the swelter of the Mississippi Summer sun as well as the rain and hail of the Fall.

She went on…..

"After my husband died I plowed these fields with old Bessie, just like I was a man. My God was always with me and he saw us through."

She said, "God answers prayers you know" as we returned to the car.

"My husband fought to hold onto the seven acres we had here.

My promise to myself was to hold on to it as long as God willed."

Chapter 2

Him

Him

Born black and poor in the shadows of the steel mills of Gary, Indiana, simply surviving life, in retrospect, feels like a major achievement. The 50's and 60's in Gary, Indiana was a smorgasbord of crime, racism, poverty, transition and opportunity – depending on who you were.

As the son of a loving, single parent, in a matriarchal home environment, avoiding the legacy of what many describe as ………………

…."black male destructionism"…. has been a challenge bigger than life.

Escaping the spiral of demise for me, my sons and my daughters started firstly with an acceptance that… the spiral exists… and understanding how my father's past and my own past come together to form who I am and who my son's and daughter's "may be"… as a result.

Beyond the understanding… are the feelings. Little did I know how those feelings got there or what the feelings were — neither did I know what to do with them when I gained the strength to get in touch with them.

My work, which has been a major source of learning for me, was the avenue through which I learned the initial lesson that resulted in a significant growth experience for me. It was at work, that a man (Steve), after being terminated, told me that he had come to "forgive" the boss that fired him.

It was the reference to "forgiveness" that had a kind of awakening affect on me. The word sounded so foreign to me in the workplace, yet quite appropriate. Beyond it's under-developed application in the workplace the word touched something in me that I didn't truly discover until several weeks later.

The realization hit me like a Mack truck at 8:00 am on a winding stretch of a central New Jersey country road on the way to work. This time the word "forgiveness," secretly imbedded in a quiet song on my car radio, loudly screamed my name and put me in touch with an important piece of unfinished business between my father and me.

"I had not forgiven him."

My father left my mother before I was born. I held this against him and after 40 years of life, 40 years of untapped anger, 40 years of unresolved frustration, 40 years of missed opportunity, 40 years of pain and 40 years of hurt, I needed to let it go. I had to let it go.

I had to let it go for me. I had to let it go for him. I had to let it go for my sons and daughters. The weight of it all was more than I knew. Releasing the anger now was confusing yet it felt so necessary. Releasing the hurt now was scary. Releasing it all was all I could do. I couldn't hold it back. I needed to free myself…. And…. I did.

My freedom came in tears. The freedom and the forgiveness were tied inextricably together.

The tears provided a cleansing relief to my eyes and to my inner-soul. These "undiscovered tears" quenched the fire that burned undetected inside of me.

The tears became a kind of eraser for the long yet unspoken list I kept hidden inside. Now, the list of transgressions was being erased one by one, tear by tear.

The cleansing process, the torrent, lasted as long as it was necessary. I wasn't in control. My inner-soul was getting what it needed and there was nothing I could do to stop it. It felt great. It was refreshing to me.

I wondered…"how did I get to this place?"

The question begged for a response, an answer of some sort. For the first time I could look at the situation freely.

I had to realize what ....really "wasn't".... in order to understand what ...really "is".... the "truth" behind my condition.

The sky was clear and the sun shined with the same warmth that I felt that child-like morning when I felt so all alone, yet somehow embraced by the glow and power of being alive. I was six then, today I'm 55.

He was alive then even though somehow it didn't seem to matter.

He's dead now, and somehow, again .... it doesn't seem to matter.

While the sadness of it all was a feeling too far away to reach at the time, today the sadness looms over me, in me and between. Between those days, those empty days of missed opportunity and undiscovered pain — all there was to being alive, was being me. A morning in the sun, crouched next to "the neighbor's" garage, huddled, knees against my chest, facing the sun as it radiates, even through my closed eyelids... defined an "embrace" for me.

I never knew his embrace. He never knew mine.

I came to know his pain. He never knew mine.

I forgave him even though he never knew my hurt or the "faults" I accused him of. I never felt the hug I never knew I needed. It passed me by and sealed itself in a small ceremonial urn I just couldn't bare to hold.

Standing there, with my brothers and sisters, the six of us seemed, to a degree, untouched by the moment. We had traveled from the four corners of the country to be there. We had spontaneously agreed that being there was the right thing to do. Yet standing there, left us all somehow struggling with what to say, how to behave, what to feel... if to feel.

We've been to funerals. We've seen families cry. We've seen the pain from the loss. Where is ours? Who, what, when, where, how were we robbed of this right, this privilege? The answers weren't there.

My eyes were void of the tears as I reflected on the memory of the man. Being there was a necessary and right thing to do. We were good at doing "the right thing," that was one of the few things he gave me along with two driving lessons and a summer job in 1969.

Reflecting on it now, as a matter of fact, he gave all those things to me in the same summer of 1969. Mom must have talked to him. I have no other explanation for such an outpouring of benevolence after 18 years of nothing. One of those trips home from work that summer included the famous "right & wrong" speech. It went something like this, "Son, if you don't know anything else, know the difference between right and wrong. You may not always do right, but always know the difference between right and wrong." Well, as I heard it, it sounded stupid. I always laughed inside whenever I repeated it to myself. I would tell my close friends the story and it never seemed as stupid to them, it never seemed to get a reaction from them one way or the other.

Today, having experienced a good part of life, somehow it doesn't seem so stupid anymore.

Somehow the words make a little sense.

Somehow this man who never knew me, knew himself well enough, knew his life experience with all its wrongs intimately enough to share it.

To share it with his youngest son, with me.

The sun was lowering in the west, through the trees that outlined the perimeter of the cemetery as we walked from the crematory. The urn the caretaker gave us had an eerie sort of air to it as my older brother, Chuck, held it close to his chest. He always seemed to express a kind of fondness for him I never understood. My oldest sister, Dottie, always "stately" in her demeanor, leaned in toward Chuck as the question of who would be the "keeper" drifted between them. They both agreed to take the urn to Texas where they both lived.

Denise, Debbie, Sonny and I didn't challenge the decision. Nobody ever questioned our silence. We were the only ones there.... the six of us. Not his brothers, not his friends, not our mom nor the other woman in his life. Mom would call her "cat eyes." That's all we knew of her, not her name, first or last, nothing but a reference to her eyes. The reference to her eyes always made me want to see them. I assumed they were green. The reference gave her a kind of mysterious persona. My curiosity was never satisfied. She wasn't there either.

Mom wasn't there. We never asked why, but we all understood. I guess anyone would.

They had separated over 40 years ago.

I learned about their separation at some point in my early childhood development, but I don't remember when. It was just ..."the way it was."

It was always that way.

I learned early on that being a father didn't mean you had to live with your children. He was my father. I knew it because everybody knew it. Especially on Sundays and holidays.

On Sundays we'd pass him on the street corner of 25th and Polk Streets. All the streets were named after dead presidents which somehow gave a bit of irony to the crowd that always gathered there from Friday night to Sunday afternoon to bend elbows with cheap wine, bad whiskey and bold tales.

It was never a surprise to us that the crowd would frequently call him a liar when he would claim to them that "those are my kids" when we would pass in our Sunday best. We'd let him argue it out with them for a few minutes before we'd finally tell them he wasn't lying. As the crowd would smile and shower him and us with compliments we knew that it made him proud... deserving or not.

14

In a strange way it made us feel good too. I guess "allowing" him to bask in the glow of the moment with his friends was his reward for just being our father.

How could we deny him that?

We could. But for some reason we never did.

It was just the way it was. We didn't ask for it to be that way. We were sure Mom didn't want it to be that way. But we never knew how it got that way, I certainly didn't. "Separated" that is.

Mom never spoke about it.

Gran always called him "Chicken."

Gran was Mom's mother, our grandmother. She was always there, she lived with us. We never knew what she did to contribute to the family, but she was always there. Maybe that was what she did, "just be there." I assumed she had always been there. I mean from the start. You know, always, like forever or the beginning of time. I couldn't remember when her long gray hair, high cheekbones and pointed nose weren't around.

She was the daughter of an Indian Princess that married an ex-slave in Mississippi. She was full of energy and as much a part of life for us as Mom was.

She was such a part of life that when she said something with conviction we listened. A strong devout Christian she was.

She always referred to him as "Chicken" with conviction, and we always heard it.

By the time he died I had discovered why Gran called him "Chicken." Looking back I don't know why it took so long for me to figure it out. What else would you expect a loving mother to call a man who walks away from "her daughter" (his wife) and child only to pursue his own drunkenness and continually return to father five more children. Over the course of 16 years, while all along not providing an ounce of support, in retrospect, "Chicken" was probably the worst name that the God in her would allow her to use.

But Mom loved him.

Despite her mother's disapproval, Mom loved him. I'm sure she loved him until the day he died.

It must have been tough for her not to be there. I'm sure it would have been even tougher for her to be there. She never told me that, somehow I just knew it.

Somehow I knew that the love and the hurt must have struggled inside her. A struggle she must have come to know all too well. A struggle that like an enemy faced over and over, in some cruel way becomes a kind of companion.

We didn't talk about these things. We didn't think to ask, Mom didn't chose to offer. Life was to be lived. Work and school consumed the week, and Church and play consumed the weekend. Life centered around the positives of family not the negatives. God knows, if we wanted to, we had enough negatives to go around, but Mom and Gran insulated us from them all.

….Even from "Him".

Their love surrounded us.

Their love covered up for the one bedroom that housed seven people. Gran had a bedroom to herself. The love between mother and daughter managed to stretch Mom's meager seamstress salary of $4,000 a year far enough to feed and clothe all eight of us. Gran was on social security, her money, whatever she got, was her's.

Mom and Gran insulated and provided for us all right. Mostly Mom. Nobody could ever say that Mom didn't take responsibility for her children. Having children may not have been the "right" thing for a single parent to do but she never made it anybody's problem but her own.

That same ownership and responsibility probably helped her deal with her relationship with him. It was nobody's problem but her own. If she could deal with his absence, his presence, absence, presence and absence again, she could deal with its outcomes and everything that came with it.

She did….. everyday, as she cared for us.

As the sun went down at the gravesite that afternoon we returned to 2575 Jefferson Street. And faded into family. We drifted into the comfortable realm of Mom and Gran.

Gran had outlived him.

I'm sure she felt some level of relief, if only in knowing that he couldn't invade her space anymore. Knowing that he had come and gone for the last time must have been the source of some strange form of relief for us all, ….. but we'd never say it.

As we stood in those same spaces we grew from, words seemed to escape us. The traditional stories told about family passed away was absent from this arena. We'd never gotten good at this anyway. We had been fortunate or blessed in our experience with death. Gran was over 100 and still going strong. When "Big Uncle Nelson" passed away early, he left a long legacy of stories, experiences with us and his children, so it was easy to come up with positive words to help pass the pain.

In this case the words weren't there.

Neither was the pain.

Somehow, being back in the home he never knew, back with people he never knew, made it somehow seem okay to let it pass…. to let the event pass.

To move past the event and back to family came more quickly than he would come on those Sunday afternoons when he'd just show up drunk, and then …. "disappear", again.

No one dried their tears, there weren't any.

No one glanced at his pictures on the wall, there weren't any.

No one spoke of their favorite story of him. Those stories don't exist for us. We never heard them. He never shared them. He wasn't really a part of our world.

What we didn't know was the extent to which he really may be a part of us internally.

It's only now that I have begun to realize the things that he has shared, with me. With me for sure, with my brothers probably and with my sisters... I'm afraid.

A confirmation that it is easier to take flight in a marriage than it is to look at self, find alternative approaches to "work it out" and "stay". It's easier to search for a "better relationship" or gain more "control", when the tougher task is to look at self and choose to change. It's easier for us and our partners to point the finger of blame in the opposite direction instead of focusing the arrow into ourselves.

Like "HIM".... like us.... like me, ..."how far from the tree does the apple fall?"

Chapter 3

Choosing to Live

Choosing to Live

Being born the child of Frances Hill, choosing to live seemed inherited by my brothers, sisters and me. Day to day as we grew in Gary, Indiana, 2575 Jefferson Street, Broadway, 25th Avenue, Douglass Elementary School, Gary Roosevelt High School, Van Buren and Adams Street all seemed to be our home and our safety zone.

We traversed these areas streets and spaces in comfort as we continued to grow-up, learn, survive and develop in the life available to us. Each year, each month, each season, each year, we were aware of choices that life had dealt us. We were aware more and more as we grew that the life choices we made would make the critical difference in our lives, our future and our happiness.

The fall night had slowly draped itself over our meager campsite. It had taken us about an hour to get there, from the Van Buren Baptist Church parking lot, across the tracks, through the small rural town and around the big red barn that the owner of the farm positioned between his house and the woods, to where we were given permission to camp for the weekend. On the way through town a few of the young Scouts, our little brothers, noticed a General Store and expressed a desire to return later to buy some "stuff." As President of the Explorer Scout Troop, I told them "no." Roy, my VP and best buddy supported my "no". We thought that would end it. It didn't, ….. despite our threats of bodily harm.

As we lay sleeping that first night I was awakened by the sounds of a muffled thud against the tent wall. Then another, and another. As other members awakened to the same sound, Roy said "someone is throwing at the tent." Jeffrey said yes and they are throwing eggs. The stain of the egg was visible on the canvas tent walls as we focused a flashlight inside the tent. That's when we heard…"we see you…. nigger's… over there…!!!"

My heart raced as the reality of our circumstance whirled around inside of me. The images of "negro" lynches flashed in front of my eyes as my mind darted back and forth from fear to question, from what action to take, to how to feel or what to say. What to say to myself but also, what to say to the others. What should I tell them to do? How could I explain to their parents what had happened? How could I tell anyone about this ?

Would I even have an opportunity to tell anyone? Would anyone ever know what was about to happen? My God! What is about to happen?

I could feel my brain about to burst with the overload of unanswered questions all on top of a backdrop of the fear and the voices coming from the pitch black dark that surrounded the densely wooded campsite. I could feel my body temperature rise as the volume and accelerated speed of emotion and thought raced inside my head and heart at the same time. The voices rang out with an insidious monotone over and over, again and again. The words, "that word", was now also pounding in my mind and emotions along with the fear and indecision.

That "word " …"nigger".

That indignation jumped from the short sentences that contained it, leaving a lasting… "bitter after taste" that I had never experienced before. Now I knew what my mother must have felt that day, standing at the bus stop on her way home from work.

As we lay sleeping that first night I was awakened by the sounds of a muffled thud against the tent wall. Then another, and another. As other members awakened to the same sound, Roy said "someone is throwing at the tent." Jeffrey said yes and they are throwing eggs. The stain of the egg was visible on the canvas tent walls as we focused a flashlight inside the tent. That's when we heard..."we see you.... nigger's... over there...!!!"

My heart raced as the reality of our circumstance whirled around inside of me. The images of "negro" lynches flashed in front of my eyes as my mind darted back and forth from fear to question, from what action to take, to how to feel or what to say. What to say to myself but also, what to say to the others. What should I tell them to do? How could I explain to their parents what had happened? How could I tell anyone about this ?

Would I even have an opportunity to tell anyone? Would anyone ever know what was about to happen? My God! What is about to happen?

I could feel my brain about to burst with the overload of unanswered questions all on top of a backdrop of the fear and the voices coming from the pitch black dark that surrounded the densely wooded campsite. I could feel my body temperature rise as the volume and accelerated speed of emotion and thought raced inside my head and heart at the same time. The voices rang out with an insidious monotone over and over, again and again. The words, "that word", was now also pounding in my mind and emotions along with the fear and indecision.

That "word " ..."nigger".

That indignation jumped from the short sentences that contained it, leaving a lasting... "bitter after taste" that I had never experienced before. Now I knew what my mother must have felt that day, standing at the bus stop on her way home from work.

Mom was dedicated to her work. Like the sunrise, she was dependable and "up and at it" early every morning, come rain or shine. She walked the 3 to 5 miles one way everyday like clock work and without complaint or she took the bus when she could. Her dedication to providing for her family was the driving force for her willingness to take risks and put herself in harms way, making the attack on her pride and well-being even more painful for me.

As she stood at the bus stop on the corner by the Cleaners where she worked, a car filled with young white men passed by and shouted racial slurs at her. A hardworking mother of six, dedicated employee, tax paying citizen, GOD fearing believer, innocent on all counts, finds herself assaulted for no reason other than the color of her skin. Ironically, it's possible that on that same day, in her job, she may have been repairing the clothes for the parents of those self-same verbal attackers.

To them she was just a "nigger" in "their part of town". Just a "nigger" standing on a corner. Just a "nigger"!!!

Well, I beg to differ. My mother is wonderful on every front. She has always inspired and encouraged others.

She overcame all kinds of odds and adversities. When she came home that night, I could tell that she was hurt, but not afraid. Hurt, but not angry. Hurt but not disenchanted or discouraged. For me, I was both proud of her strength and resilience, while also angered to a boiling point. I wanted to hit someone, hit back and somehow have them feel the pain.

Again we heard it ……

"We see you niggers over there!!!"….. "You can't hide niggers!!!"

As those words rang out once more, something came over me.

Something came over my…. fear. Something jolted my mind.

Something inside sprang through the heat of the moment to answer my questions, to resolve my indecision. Suddenly the paralysis that had imprisoned me was gone. In reality the time lapse was probably measured in seconds, but now…. I was clear.

Now…., I felt empowered to deal with the situation. If I had been asked then, "What was it that released me from my frozen state?" I wouldn't have known. Looking back on it today, the answer is clearer.

Choosing to live, choosing to survive, choosing to be respected. Choosing not to allow others to force me, outside of my will, not to force me to be afraid.

Without recognizing it, I was about to exercise my choice. I was about to choose to be free, free to stand my ground, free to be left in peace, free to fight for my right to be there…in that place, that day, that night. Free!

In retrospect, the passion and courage to thwart this threat to my freedom outweighed the fear of the unknown force or intent behind what was waiting for us outside of that tent. I imagine now that the same primal rage that welled in my ancestors, as they were captured and transported to the New World, welled up in me that night. The combination of rage, and the right of self-defense spawned a new clarity of mind for me. Looking inward at myself I reaffirmed my responsibility as a leader of the group and deployed my plan.

As I huddled the group quickly together, my plan was founded on our only advantage. Surprise. I told the group in muffled tone, that………. "the last thing these guys expect is for us to attack them."

A moment of shocked silence fell over the tent. I knew some of them were saying to themselves "…is he crazy?!" Sure, they had no idea how many of them were out there. Of course, they could be armed with guns, knives, clubs, who knows what. With conviction I pushed back… "and, they have no idea how many of us there are either," I said. "Nor do they know whether we have weapons or not. " I implored, "…trust me, they will never expect us to rush them. Let's grab our axes, knives, bows and arrows, anything we have. We'll slide out of the tent, down toward the embankment. When I yell, 'Charge!' I want everyone to jump up screaming at the top of your voice, and rush toward them. I want you to yell, curse, and growl as you run head-on into whoever is out there.

Trust me, they will run, shocked and disoriented. They will have to split up due to the trees. If you catch one or not, yell out as if you have caught one. Yell things like, 'I got one y'all, should I kill him?' Scream and whack the trees or create any noise you can."

As we slid out of the tent, we heard "those words" once again. As we settled down and poised ourselves to pounce from the embankment, we could see some of the moon's glow on their pale skin and their button's reflections glistened through the trees.

Again we heard…"we see you niggers over there." Twice, three times and then, four. Before the last word allowed their tongues to retreat behind their "cheshire" teeth, I gave the order …and… in unison we sprang forward like banshees from Hades. Brandishing our wood axes, knives, bows, sticks and stones…. the attackers were turned on their heels. The hunters, the attackers, instantly converted to the prey, the victims. It was a sight to see, the sounds were those of deer or cattle crashing through thicket. Ahead of us we could barely see, but mostly hear them and they slammed into the brush and trees as they outran our screams. We pursued them "alleging captures" and asking permission to kill our "make-believe" victims. We could hear them screaming to each other, "run" "no this way" "where is Tommy?" "did you see Johnny?" over and over as they fled.

Finally we called off our pursuit and huddled together to catch our breath from the exhilaration of the adrenaline rush and the spent energy. It was a brief time for celebration and acknowledgement of our victory. We had turned back the threat to our lives. We had secured our freedom to be left in peace — "to be left….. in peace", even if it was "their" part of the world. We had established a new boundary for our "right-to-be" in peace. We were now recognizing that, in fact, our "right-to-be" in peace should have no boundary. Our innocent intent should not be barred from, or limited to, prescribed boundaries. That, as human beings, as full citizens, as boys, as men — we too, had a right-to-be… a right to live. It really was our choice.

We chose to live.

Chapter 4

Grandma's Hands

Augusta Harris-Bliss

They called her "Indian Mary". Her face was bold and full of pride for who she was. There was strength to her stride as she walked; yet grace accompanied her every step. She was the daughter of a Cherokee Chief and Princess to her people who had been relocated to the southeast after the Indian Wars of the 1850s.

Indian Mary stood tall in heart and spirit among her people as they interfaced daily with whites and blacks alike.

Indian Mary married an ex-slave man named Nelson Bliss in the 1850's in Indianola, Mississippi. They had six children of that marriage. Their names were Splender, Walter, Ernest, Turner, a little girl named Waltee and Nelson Jr. The family worked their farm in Indianola season after season. They had worked this farm for decades as freemen with full rights of citizenship. As the years rolled on, each son and the only daughter Waltee, pursued their life choices, relationships and education as deemed appropriate to them individually.

We are unable to confirm the timing or the cause, but Indian Mary passed away while Waltee was still just a child.

Nelson continued to forge ahead as Father and Mother to his sons and daughter.

Across the state of Mississippi, a man named George Harris met and married Louvenia, a sophisticated young lady of Indian heritage.

Her high cheekbones were clearly indicative of her Native American heritage. They enjoyed a long life together full of hard work and children. Children were needed to work the tough Mississippi farmland. Their marriage was a "blended family" in that they both brought a combined total of twelve children from previous marriages into this new family of fourteen.

On December 11, 1884, a beautiful fair skinned baby girl was born to them in Starkville, Oktibeha County, Mississippi. They named her Augusta. She was now added to the twelve other children these middle aged parents already had from their previous marriages. Augusta Harris was full of life and wore her Indian and African heritage with pride. She struck an impressive pose as she sat bareback atop the Appaloosa mare they called Sparkle. She attended New Bethel School at a young age, escorted on the arm of her brother Lee. She knew the alphabet and was knowledgeable about a long list of subjects when she entered New Bethel School. This was in stark contrast to her father who could recite the letters of the alphabet but couldn't read. Augusta was struck with the whooping cough after her first two weeks in school and missed the remainder of the school year due to her illness. In those days (1891-1892) a school term lasted only four months, from November to early March.

Augusta was exceedingly smart and often received honors, being referred to as "The Walking Dictionary" by her classmates. As a teenager Augusta was quite petite and shapely with the long, black hair traditional to the Cherokee. Her high cheekbones and fair skin were accented by wide dark eyes separated by a wide nose reminiscent of the African and Native American blood that flowed in her veins.

At the age of seventeen Augusta was selected by the County Superintendent to hold the position of Principal of a small school in Phebe, Mississippi. She finished her high school education at New Prospect School, was tested by the state and received her License to become the Principal of Phebe School. She walked three miles everyday from Starkville to Phebe to serve as Principal and to teach.

After several years as Principal at Phebe she returned to New Prospect School and became a Teacher's Assistant.

Augusta was full of life and anxious to grow up in the early 1900's rural Mississippi. In 1909, she traveled from Starkville to Indianola to visit her sister. It didn't take long for "suitors" to come calling. The "suitor" that got her attention was Nelson Bliss Jr., a handsome young man, marked by his full head of dark black hair separated down the middle with a well groomed "part". Augusta was twenty-five years old and marriage was soon to follow their short courtship. She accepted Christ as her personal Savior in 1910 at the Church of Christ Holiness in Indianola and became Secretary of the Sunday School, a role she retained for several years.

Nine years after marriage the couple had their first child, Mae Frances. Augusta's mother, Luvenia passed away four months later. Augusta was proud to be the wife of Nelson Bliss Jr. He was a good man, father and husband for.....years. As the years moved on Augusta and Nelson had three more children, Harris Nathaniel, Nelson and Merline Vanetta. Nelson struggled early in the marriage with a disabling disease, of an unknown origin, that made his legs weaker, susceptible to frequent breakage and leading eventually to life in a wheelchair and an early death in 1930. His passing had left Augusta with four children and a large plot of land that required a lot of hard work to maintain. She worked the fields, cared for the children and held on to a strong belief in GOD and the importance of creating a future for them all.

One evening, the Lord spoke to Augusta in a dream and instructed her to leave Mississippi and take her children "up north" for better opportunity, to GOD's Country as she had called it for years. It was 1937 when she told her oldest child Frances about her goal. She had discussed it over and over with her late husband, now departed, but he had said it was "too cold" for him "up there in the North". After his passing there was no reason to hold back her vision.

However, her dream had to wait. The family worked the land and grew individually and collectively over the years to come. World War II saw the enlistment of both sons into the Army.

On November 2, 1942 her eldest child, Frances at the age of 23, left Indianola, headed...."up North"...to Gary, Indiana.

Gary was known as a STEEL TOWN, with the promise of good, solid work in the steel mills that outlined the southern shores of Lake Michigan. The stories of "black folks" from the south finding good jobs and building nice homes was as much in the news as World War II. Frances packed her meager belongings and posed for pictures with the family in front of their farmhouse before heading "North", toward a promise of a better life for her family. A better life that her mother Augusta had longed for since 1927. The dream she had about better opportunities for her brothers Harris and Nelson and her sister Merline. The North held the promise for them all. It was Frances' responsibility to find a job and find a temporary home for the family that would follow later.

In February 1943 the rest of the family traveled North to join Frances in Gary, Indiana. The family's move to the North was reminiscent of the Native American's constant relocation across the country in search of fertile ground and good hunting. Their drive to move to a place where the opportunity to prosper and provide for themselves mirrored the Gold Rush days of the 1840s. Pursuit of the promises that this "land of the free and the brave" had to offer was a vision Augusta held close to her heart for decades.

The "opportunity" had become a "reality" as the Bliss Family arrived in Gary, Indiana. Frances had preceded them and had been successful in finding work as well as a place to live. The Church that they had been members of in Mississippi had a Gary affiliate, Christ Temple Holiness Church had rented her a small bungalow behind the Church at very little expense.

In the late winter of 1943 the brothers, sister and mother arrived in Gary to begin their new lives in the "promised land" of opportunity via the Steel Mills.

Over the years following, each brother and her sister found jobs in the Steel Mills, got married, found homes for themselves and began to live the life that "moving North" had promised. Harris and Nelson began to have children. Merline married her husband yet they had no children. Frances had been the first to marry after she was introduced by "Church folks" to a handsome young man with a history of drinking and misbehaving. However, his charm won her over. They married and had six children but spent very little time together as husband and wife over the course of 30 years.

Gran rose early every morning as the sun came up. Quietly in her room she kneeled at her bedside to pray. In her room was the air of a sanctuary during her time of prayer. Everyone in the house knew not to disturb Gran as she prayed. Somehow, to my young eyes it seemed like her prayer time would last all morning long.

Captain Kangaroo would come and go before she would arise from the quietness of her room. Her prayer time was followed by reading the Bible off and on all day long, everyday.

As a boy growing up in Gary, Indiana, Gran was a constant figure of respect and love. We knew she loved us in everything she'd do and say. We knew her daily prayers covered our Mother, Frances and each of us. We knew her actions and comments were designed to support our growth and development. I can hear her now as she would always admonish me, in the heat of our summer, as she would yell at the top of her voice…."Boy, put a hat on yo' head, you gonna get "black as coal."

Well, she was a fair-skinned woman and after 80 years of life in the South, her life experience had proven that being "black as coal" was a disadvantage. Her whole reason for "coming North" was to get away from disadvantages for her children. Surely, her heart held the same concern for her grandchildren, for me.

My Grandmother's love for us was evident in everything she did…. and didn't do. Gran was always there. We knew we could depend on her to be available in the house if we ever needed her. We knew that as our Mother walked to work everyday, Gran was there for us. As we played in the alleys or in the street, Gran was always at home to mend our knees.

Gran was there when we fell from trees. Gran was there in Winter, Summer, Spring and Fall. Gran was always there when we got big and when we were small.

Our Grandmother was a "mother" in some ways, in the home and Church. In the home she "mothered" us as our Mother worked like a Father to supply all of our needs. In the Church, our Gran was appointed a "Mother of the Church" due to the strength of her spirituality and relationship with God. Her strength and convictions led her to stand for truth as she knew it and to confront wrong anywhere she saw it.

One of those "wrongs" was my Father, my Mothers estranged husband.

Mae Frances Bliss-Hill

While my mother, Frances, loved him, Gran despised the man for abandoning his wife and children.

She despised him even more for showing-up at our (her) front door weekend after weekend, year after year, child after child, decade after decade….drunk… and under the influence of alcohol. I remember vividly his showing-up one Sunday and locking himself in the bedroom. Gran was so upset after demanding him to leave that she proceeded to sweep buckets of water underneath the bedroom door…in an effort to "flush" him out of the house. Water was everywhere…!!! She screamed… "Demon, get out of this house…!!!" …. over and over again. After a couple of hours, he finally walked out… never to enter our home again.

Frances and Mansfield Hill Sr. continued to struggled to be husband and wife as the combination of his alcoholism, separation and her Mother Augusta refused to step out of the equation.

Mansfield had chosen to be a slave to alcohol.

Frances had chosen to live… secure with her children and her Mother Augusta, free from alcohol and irresponsibility. She chose to live with the responsibility for her children and her Mother. Frances had chosen to secure a life full of promise and opportunity for her children rather than a life of alcohol, excuses and unhealthy life choices and examples.

Frances had chosen to live in freedom rather than fall into the promise of slavery through alcoholism and irresponsibility.

She had chosen to live.

Frances had chosen to live…. free, free of a possessive relationship with the man she had loved for forty years. The only man she had ever loved.

She had chosen to live free …. and remain free of any subsequent "possessions" by any other man. Her freedom also strengthened her loving indebtedness to the family she had created. It served to solidify her committed sacrifices to the children she had brought into this world. Her freedom somehow accelerated the fuel that fed the love and devotion she held for us all. The six of us, yes, even the seven of us counting our Grandmother, languished in the full devotion of our Mother, her daughter. Gone now was the expectation that "he" would show up every weekend… drunk.

She remained steadfast in her devotion to us. She worked hard everyday at the Cleaners where she served as Seamstress.

Frances had followed in the footsteps that hundreds of other African American Women had forged before her. She continued to manage to secure the small space she had in this house at 2575 Jefferson Street.

Over the years and decades to follow, Frances continued to forge an existence for her children and her Mother at 2575 Jefferson Street, within walking distance of Christ Temple Holiness Church.

Walking distance was important because neither of them were able to drive a car, not to mention...afford one. So walking is what we did. We walked to Church two or three times a week, rain, sleet, snow or sunshine... with up to six children and a Grandmother in tow. Sunday was Sunday School and Church Service, then there was Choir Rehearsal and HBU (Holiness Bible Union). Every summer there was Vacation Bible School and often the Summer Excursion to Chicago to hear Billy Graham at Soldiers Field or attend a Holiness Church Convention. The memories of those huge events resonate in my mind's eye as if it were yesterday. The smell and taste of fried chicken and potato salad in picnic baskets, the thought of homemade pound cake, homemade ice cream and soda pop bring back a vision of a simpler life, a life full of "Family" and a focus on "God" and "love" for one another.

The homemade ice cream became a sort of "summer ritual". This was a time when the meaning of "process management" was so fundamental and natural. The word "process" never came to mind. It just happened...!!!

The process started when Frances decided she wanted homemade ice cream.....usually a hot summer's Sunday afternoon. Her determination was followed by a dozen egg yolks, vanilla, milk, sugar, a bunch of rock salt, a block of ice, a manual ice cream maker consisting of a large wooden pail with a stainless steel inner cylinder, a paddle mixer, a crank and the muscle of four children. I was number four.

The process started with Frances mixing and slowly cooking all of the ingredients. While they cooked, the mixer was cleaned and ice placed around the stainless steel inner-cylinder. After cooling, the cylinder was filled, the crank installed and secured in place. The ice and salt was poured around the cylinder in the pail and then it was time for the cranking to begin.

The youngest of the four children (me) would crank first because it was easier and less resistance while the liquid ice cream spun inside the steel cylinder. As the resistance increased, the next oldest child took over the cranking. At the next point of resistance each older child took over until the ice cream was in fact frozen to a smooth custard peak. It moved from Edwin to Doris to Cornell to Mansfield and Frances always turned the crank a few more times to "finish if off"...to perfection.

The whole family watched as she lifted the paddles from the steel cylinder and carefully scrapped the frozen custard from each paddle and blade down into the cylinder. It was the height of my desire to be the one given that paddle...to lick every drop of ice cream from each nook and cranny.

For me, the culmination of that "process" was well worth the patience, time investment, teamwork and individual effort. The outcome and value added of that "process" was obvious to each one of us.

In retrospect, there were any number of other life experiences and examples like this one for my family. The bi-weekly grocery shopping process, the daily winter "coal gathering" process, the Saturday clothes washing process, the Family bathing process the weekly meal planning process and on and on, were all the result of my Mother Mae Frances Bliss-Hill "finding a way" to make life secure and comfortable for six children and our Grandmother, in a two bedroom bungalow, on one small income. Today, I have one of her weekly check-stubs from 1961 reflecting a total of $44.61. She met all of the needs of eight people on less than $50.00 a week.

Frances continued to support and strengthen her family at 2575 Jefferson Street, year after year, decade after decade. On her small income she continued to feed and clothe six children, she continued to keep a roof over our heads and good meals on the table. Frances made acquiring a good public school education a requirement, she urged each child to pursue any gift they desired, including piano, singing, cheerleading, athletics and art. In addition, she encouraged each child to participate in Church, social and civic activities, including band, sports, bible study, Boy Scouts and neighborhood activities. She also set a fine example as she engaged and joined in many of these activities as best she could despite her limited access to transportation.

As each child grew to early adulthood, Frances was there to encourage and support us. Mansfield Jr.'s decision to join the Navy, our first lovers and our children born out of wedlock were fully embraced loved and cared for by our Mother, Frances. My choice to go away to College without complete financial support or assistance was encouraged. My sister Denise's choice for marriage and children at 18 after a stellar High School experience was also embraced and supported.

Simultaneous to the evolution of her children, other family members and friends continued to evolve as Frances stood tall in their support. Whether it was divorce, abuse, re-marriage, financial challenges, emotional support or just a caring ear, Frances Hill...was always "there" ....for family, neighbors and friends.

Her support and "being there" for me is highlighted in my heart when she traveled from Indiana to Baltimore and Pennsylvania in 1999 to be with me in my battle with bone marrow cancer. No, this was not just your traditional visit or vacation trip. This trip emphasized again her love for me. Sure, every Mother is expected to love her son. Every son is expected to love his Mother. However, most Mother to Son relationships go un-tested and un-challenged for the true meaning in those relationships. Most Mother and Son relationships are void of trials, travails, tribulations, highpoints or highlights like the one we share. On one hand, those Mothers and Sons are blessed to not have this common bond with us. On the other hand, they can't imagine the "bliss", benevolence and pride I've experienced in "sharing life"...because of my Mother and "with" my Mother.

I can only "try" to put this into words as I reference "choosing life over death".

You see, my Mother "chose" to bring me into life. However, recently she shared with the Family that she struggled with the choice to bring my younger sisters Denise and Debbie Jo into the world. In fact she considered abortion in both cases. Her "choosing life over death" in both circumstances has and will continue to have mind-boggling impact on my life, her life and countless other Family members and other unrelated individuals that our lives touch.

In the past few years the following events have occurred as a result of Frances' choosing to bring both Denise and Debbie Jo to life.

1. Denise mothered 9 children, 6 boys and 3 girls. What life holds for them and their children has yet to fully unfold.

2. In addition to bringing 9 children into the world, Denise was the bone marrow donor for my cancer therapy and transplant in 1999.

3. Debbie Jo relocated both our Mother Frances and our Aunt Merline from Gary, Indiana to Houston, Texas to avoid the cold winters.

4. My wife Brenda and I assisted Denise and her husband Melvin in purchasing a new home out of inner-city Indianapolis, thereby creating a much healthier environment for them to raise and educate their six youngest children.

5. Brenda and I purchased a home in the Houston area to allow Frances and Merline to relocate from the cold of Northwest Indiana and be closer to our sister Doris for support while also providing shelter for my brother Cornell as their new care-giver.

Only God knows what's next as we pursue his will in our lives and as we follow the footsteps of Mae Frances Bliss-Hill … my Mother.

{Photograph: Augusta (seated) surrounded by (left to right) Frances, Harris, Nelson and Merline}

Chapter 5

The Neighborhood: Sons of the City

The Neighborhood:

The streets were paved in red cobblestone, polished smooth by years of traffic.

So what, we didn't have a car. We didn't miss it or didn't know what we were missing. In either case, cars weren't important to me. What was important was the huge white horse that pulled the wooden wagon filled with fresh fruit and vegetables which made a frequent summer pass through the neighborhood. The driver, a bronze-colored leathery-skinned man, weathered by the labor and sun, would yell "waaatermelonnnn, get your red ripe waaatermelonnnn!!!" at the top of his lungs. That sound would send us all running to the edge of the street to watch them pass.

The horse and the man were like a team, seemingly formed out of need and love for one another. The horse was tall and strong, making the man seem powerful in my eyes. The man was stern in countenance and silent, save for a low toned "giddy-up" when it was time to move on. We'd follow the team to the corner imitating the driver's refrain "waaatermelonnn!!!" and wishing we could hitch a ride.

The old black potbellied coal stove seemed to come alive when it was aglow with the red hot fire that was its winter trademark. The stove was both an enemy and a friend to me and it was the center of our world at 2575 Jefferson Street.

The daily winter chore of hauling coal from the coal bin was assigned to my oldest brother when I was too young. Gas and oil heat had already become the standard on the "other side of the tracks" but I didn't know that at the time.

It was in front of that stove that Mom and Gran would place the galvanized wash tub, fill it with water heated on top of that stove and place each one of us, starting always with the youngest (of course, the younger ones were supposed to be less dirty). One by one we'd cautiously step into that old tub, stand there while Mom or Gran soaped us down then dipped us in only long enough to clear the suds from our bottoms. Then with a warm towel, from its huddled place in front of that stove and a pat on the butt, off we'd go to the bedroom to dry and dress. That tub of water would last through the six of us, then Mom would heat it up one more time for herself.

That old pot bellied stove would lure you to it on those hard cold northern Indiana winter nights, yet it would dare you to get too close. On a good night, that stove would get white hot and keep the bulk of the four room brick bungalow moderately warm through the night. Those of us that ventured too close just might find ourselves severely fried. Being adventurous as a child, my right forearm bears the scar that is my reminder to this day of the seriousness of that stove. The stove was also a dear friend. Cast iron pressing irons were placed on it in the evening so that Mom or Gran could wrap them in towels and place them at our feet to keep us warm on the regularly bitter winter nights. The heat would keep us warm until we fell asleep. Sleep was good, unless another brother or sister shoved their toes up your nose …. while sleeping up to five of us in one bed.

But life was good. At least we thought it was.

Everything was relative. Relative to everything I knew, life was good. I was happy, my siblings were happy and Mom and Gran took care of our basic needs. Going to Church and Sunday School every Sunday was one of those "basic" things … we just did. It was a twelve block walk in our best clothes and shoes.

Gran could do wonders with the school shoes that had holes in the bottom. She would keep a supply of cardboard from boxes and cut patches in the same shape of our shoe and slide it inside. When the sole of the shoe would separate from the upper section she'd take some baling wire she saved from year to year and an ice pick and sew the halves back together. She was like a mechanic and a shoemaker all rolled into one.

If you were careful how you walked, no one would ever know your shoes were falling apart. This was much better than that dragging, "scrapping" sound and "flip-flop" noise the tattered loose sole would make. The cardboard would keep your feet dry for several days … if it didn't rain. The wire would last a week or two and was usually the last attempt at prolonging the life of the shoes before mom had saved enough to buy us a new pair of shoes.

New shoes were a mixed blessing. On one hand we were glad to escape that temporary period of embarrassment. On the other hand we had to suffer the short-lived ridicule of "the boys" in the neighborhood, probably a result of jealously, but always a pain. The aim of all your friends was to help you scuff those new shoes from top to bottom as soon as possible.

What the boys thought was important. What "the boys" thought was right and true. It was important to look good and be strong in the eyes of the boys in the neighborhood.

The alleys were a special place for us "boys" and we never seemed to mind the cinders and gravel surface that was its make-up. Down the alley to the north was "the projects," five three-story apartment buildings with wooden stairways and porches that lead to each apartment. The projects were known to house drunks and the sort of people good folks didn't spend time with, but we had friends there.

The image was always of dried out cheerios and grains of rice stuck like hundreds of desert islands in little beds of glue to the kitchen table, encased in their own sticky pond of government-issue dried milk and too much sugar. The sink and cabinet tops seemed to come alive through the scurrying back and forth of tens of roaches when we entered the room. The back door allowed just enough light into the room to illuminate the emptiness of the apartments that our friends called home.

In these projects, wonder bread, a five pound loaf of government cheese and a jar of grape jelly could bring a smile to their faces as they offered to share lunch with my brother and me. We always refused. We knew that things were worse for them than for us and we were taught not to take from others in need. We never talked about it then. Somehow things seemed worse for them, yet, there were two adults in most of those homes. This didn't always mean "husband and wife". This didn't always mean "Mother and Father". Most times it was "different".

The project buildings were three floors of apartments, four apartments to each floor, fronting on Adams Street and back facing the alley between Adams and Jefferson Streets. There were five of these buildings separated by a 4-foot wide concrete path or "gang-way." The gangway was always dark and cool, even in the daylight. Each building shadowed the other, creating a cool haven from the summer heat and a hiding place for the residents of the project.

At night, these pitch-dark gangways were an excellent place to be assaulted, harassed or mugged, if you didn't live there.

It was also a place to "make out" if you had a girlfriend. It could also be a fun place to play "hide-and-go-seek" if you were a boy without a care in the world. There were about 25 of us care-free boys, my brothers Sonny and Cornell, our buddies, Eddie, Fred, Jo-Jo, Bobbie, Palmer, Garnett, Otha, Cornelius, Arthur Jean, Tootie, Spud, Norman, Terry, Walter, Butch, Anthony, Floyd, Ricky, Billie, Earl, Wash and me. We made the whole neighborhood, the swamp, the projects and all, a place to remember a place where you could grow and discover, lead and follow, fight, struggle and survive, fail and, succeed... if you wanted to.... and we did.

Passing the years in our neighborhood was like living out an adventure fairytale.

My brother Chuck saw to that.

Everything we did had an air of adventure to it. Places like a patch of woods and swamp that ran along the new Interstate Highway 80/94 took on names like "Sherwood Forest." A wooden shack clubhouse in our vacant lot two doors down was "Fort Apache," and my brother was always Robin Hood or Custer or some other Errol Flynn character.

I never really had a name.

It was somehow sort of good enough that I could just come along on these "adventures." Who cared that "Sherwood Forest" was really just a stretch of swamp and woods that separated the Interstate Highway 80/94 from the local Public Park and our neighborhood? It was a place of wonder and adventure for us.

I didn't have one of those hero names, but when we went on an adventure I was as much my own hero as anybody could ever be. The all day excursions in Sherwood Forest were wonderfully exciting. The site of a hawk, muskrat, beaver, turtle, lizard or frog brought a rush to my senses. The tall cottonwood and sycamore trees reached to the sky always increasing their challenge to us to climb them.

The challenge always won, the fear would always fade. Yes, we'd climb the tree. We'd all climb it. Then we'd challenge anyone that wouldn't. We'd climb and call out to one another "climb higher," never giving thought to the danger, just the adventure. After all, we were "heroes".... in our hearts.

Heroes had to have "skills in weaponry" and we were no different. Except, we made our weapons. We made them from anything we could find. Our bow was made from tree limbs hacked down in Sherwood Forest. Our arrows were some form of weed that would dry straight and tall every year in the swamps that surrounded Sherwood. Our swords were from scraps of wood found in the alleys behind our homes and nailed together with the crooked nails that always accompanied the scrap wood we found in garbage piles. Once these weapons were "forged," they would be at our sides forever (or until they broke, whichever came first).

In later years we replaced these crude weapons with "store bought" bows & arrows that improved our skill and endeared these tools even closer to us. As usual Chuck was first to get new things and I always got his old version. He always told me they were good as new. I always believed him. It never seemed to matter.

In the true spirit of warriors we honed our skills at attaining spoils and treasure from "raiding." It didn't take long for me to learn the art of "raiding." "Raiding" was, in reality, stealing. I knew that, but it didn't matter. Maybe it's because of what we were stealing. We were stealing fruit. Stealing fruit from the trees and vines of our neighbors somehow didn't seem like stealing. I guess we justified it because "it grew on trees," which is different from things people buy in our corner grocery stores. Also it was stuff people kept outside in the rain and sun, not inside their homes or garages. We just had to go in the yard or climb the tree and pick it. On top of all that, it all tasted so good.

How could it be wrong? We made it an art. The first thing to learn was where the fruit trees were.

Every kid didn't know what we knew. It took years to discover all the right locations and varieties of fruit trees and vines.

The alleys were the avenues to the spoils. Down the alley between Jefferson and Adams Streets were grapes (Concord I believe) pears, and tart pie cherries. Down the alley between Jefferson and Madison Streets were pears, a large variety of Muscat grapes, apples and Bing cherries. The alley between Madison and Monroe Streets had two of the largest pear trees in the world. These trees were so tall we could only pick up the fallen fruit from the ground and they were always bruised but delicious.

Now the prize was a "yellow" Bing cherry tree down the alley between Monroe and Jackson Streets.

These cherries were not only unusual but also they were the sweetest, most delicious cherry you ever tasted. We called them "snowball cherries."

Chuck and I would go to the greatest lengths to get to these cherries.

The challenge was increased by the fact that the tree was in the yard of one of our favorite schoolteachers. A teacher that also happened to know our Mom real well.

No, that wouldn't stop us. It only meant we had to be sure not to get caught. My last memory of that raid, and maybe my last raid ever, was on a warm summer Saturday night. That night Chuck and I decided we would stay up late, watch "Shock Theater" on Channel 9 and raid the "snowball cherries" after everyone had surely gone to sleep. It must have been two o'clock in the morning, but we felt refreshed, energized and ready to go. It was a moon bright night and the air was still. We must have floated to that cherry tree because I didn't recall the trip. When we got there the spotlight from the house to the garage shined brightly and when combined with the glow of the moon it was almost as clear as day. We stood there in confidence and resolve, bags in hand, ready to climb the fence. The chain-link fence was like a staircase to the top of the garage which sat next to the cherry tree and made an excellent roosting place from which to pick to our hearts content. It all went surprisingly well. Nothing went wrong. We sat on that garage and stood in that tree eating and picking cherries till our bellies and bags were about to burst.

Everything we knew about the sweetness and unusual flavor of these cherries bore true that night. This raid was a major success. We were proud of our success. We walked slowly home. Slow was the only way we could walk since we were weighted down both inside and out. Once at home we proudly announced our bounty to those that were still awake. As we decided to remove the pits from our cherries so as to supplement the flavor with convenience, we came to a shocking discovery.

Wrapped around the pit of every cherry we opened was a short blonde colored, brown headed WORM. You can't imagine what it feels like to reflect back on having consumed hundreds of cherries only to realize after the fact that every one was filled with it's own personal WORM.

Words cannot express the urge, the need, to vomit.

I looked at my brother, he looked at me, we looked up, down at the bags and at the bathroom door. We did the best we could to rid our bodies of what we had eaten. Only God knows how we survived. But I don't recall another raid after that night.

In an all too real, but subtle way, that night I grew. Somehow, once again, life's experience proved to be an excellent teacher. Beyond my control, beyond my power, beyond my maleness, life had molded another small part of me.

That same summer as I looked at the orange-colored sand and dirt that stretched as far as my eyes could see, in that place where once we had played the games of Robin Hood in our beloved Sherwood Forest, now, everything was changing. The tall trees were gone.

The swamp was drained and in it the fish, carp and catfish alike jumped into the sky gasping for air, only to fall back to the mud that awaited them. On that day we walked home with buckets of fish. They were there for the picking. While this meant the end to a very special place in our lives it also created a new place of discovery for boys from neighborhoods all around.

The long stretch of orange sand and dirt was a great place to play football and "hide and go seek" and to discover. A great place to be a boy.

Seemingly 20 feet high and twice as long, I marveled at the road moving equipment that scattered the sandy landscape. I had never seen real earth movers and axle grease, not to mention seeing it for the first time in such volumes. The stuff was everywhere. It smelled bad and looked bad too. With the axle grease came the huge, monster-sized vehicles it kept running. Those vehicles were a great place to climb, jump, pretend and be a boy.

A boy could be a boy, here among the trucks and the tractors but... my world was changing and I hadn't come to fully realize it.

A new six-lane highway was coming through. Interstate 80 & 94 was being born. A new pipeline through the city was challenging the age old backbone of the city, across the state, and the country. It was "steel" and concrete. Surely we didn't realize that this change was a precursor to the downturn in the steel industry that would eventually rip apart the body of this place I called home.   Gary, Indiana.

Steel was failing, the mill was slowing down, the new highway was opening routes to suburbia and things would never be the same.

Before I could grow up, before I knew it, this place was becoming a critical source of learning for me. Life was becoming something that "I had to hold on to" if I wanted to have it. If I wanted to be happy.

The changing moments of each day had forced me to become more aware somehow of life. My eyes, my mind was taking ownership of the world around me.

It was me who had to change. I had to grow up. It was the sixties.

But what did it mean? How would I do it? What should I do?

I didn't have the answers. Where would I go to get them?

Sons of the City

In July and August the blaze of the sun and the humidity pressed around our neck and shoulders as we wandered the trails and worn out roads that infiltrated the place, the neighborhood we called home. As we turned slowly through the overgrown vacant lots, apartment buildings and the neighborhood maze I was reminded of chickens roasting in an oven.

The heat never seemed to stop us from playing "cricket" in the alley behind our houses. The challenge and competition kept us going even through the heat.

The game was called "cricket." We didn't know why. What we knew was that we loved it. It always seemed strange to us that only boys on our side of town played the game. Why, we never knew. Wash and Earl were great at the game. Their hand speed and assuredness was amazing to behold. I guess being brothers helped.

Two teams of two played the game. The team on defense played kneeling behind two sets of three cans (beer cans ideally, they looked nicer) set up about ten yards apart. The offense played standing in front of the cans facing each other with 3-4 foot sticks (broomsticks, ideally axe handles or fence boards). The object for the defense was to throw or roll a 2 inch diameter rubber ball quickly toward the three cans in an effort to have the offense swing at the ball and miss, thereby knocking or bowling over the cans. The objective for the offense was to hit the ball when rolled or thrown in an effort to send the defense running after the ball while each offensive player runs from one set of cans to the other, at each rotation touching their sticks in front of the set of cans equaling one point. In the end, the first team to a previously determined number of points wins. We usually played to 15.

The length of a game was often predicted by who had to get home earliest. As I recall, the team with Wash usually won. He was good!!

Washington Bridges was his name. Cornell Wellington was another name. There was Earl and Ernest and Palmer, Floyd, Eddie, Cornelius, Fred, Edmund, Garnett, Otha, Arthur, Sonny, Bobby, Joseph, Anthony and Ed. If asked, "what's in a name?" I say nothing. Ask the parents of these "Sons of the City" and you'd be surprised what they might say.

Washington Bridges could be the name of the first Afro-American White House Chief of Staff... he's not.

Cornell Wellington could be the name of the first Afro-American to be knighted by the Queen of England... he hasn't been.

Earl, Ernest, Floyd and all the rest could be President of the United States, Govenors, Mayors or at least, own their own businesses.... They don't.

Being "Sons of the City," born into certain rights of passage, bound by certain unwritten rules, little did we know that our future was always a matter of how far we could see. A matter of what we could believe....

"we could be." Each to his own, is today what he believed he could be.

To "be all you believe you can be" is no small task for a "city son" like my boys from the neighborhood, but there is a lot to be gained in the trying. It's the trying that really counts.

Some tried and succeeded, some tried and failed, some are still trying and some never really tried. Success is a relative term. "Related to what?"..... is a good question to ask. There are complicated answers for young black men growing up in Gary, Indiana in the 1960s. It could have been very easy for some of us to define success by looking at our fathers. However, very difficult for most of us. It was difficult to do, but we could have also defined success by looking at other black husbands and fathers in our neighborhood. Only time would tell what "choices" we made for our models of success. Only the days of our lives would measure our success toward being the man we chose to see...and chose to be.

As I look back on it all, my decision to go to Indiana State University was not really a "choice" at all. For most poor kids from the inner city, going to college was not really a "choice". It wasn't even on the radar screen for most of us. It was presented to me as an idea from my high school Art Teacher Mr. Owens and Guidance Counselor Mr. Stratton. Had they not opened my eyes to "give it a try", I would never have filled-out a single application. In fact, I filled-out three or four applications to various Colleges and visited them all as part of the Upward Bound Program. There must have been 40 of us, Black High School Juniors and Seniors from inner-city Gary Roosevelt High School on a Tour Bus in 1968, headed out to visit "state supported" Universities in parts of the state that we had viewed as unsafe for us to be in after dark. Bloomington, Terre Haute and Muncie, Indiana were not known for their diversity. Sure, the Civil Rights movement was well underway. Of course we were going to the sanctity of "institutions of higher learning". But, central states were "well known" for their southern sympathies and northern dislikes.

The trip was uneventful from any racial derogatory remarks or run-ins and I walked away impressed more by the lunch menu from the Cafeterias than any other factors. Ultimately, I decided to attend the school with a good Art Program and the best food. Of course the food quality was a lot worse after I got there. In any case, I was going to have fun. I could see myself growing in confidence and comfort as I began to "create my future", a future beyond the walls of this city. I was moving toward my own vision of life beyond my past, beyond my present, beyond the traditional life of a "son" of this city.

Looking at our fathers was harder for some of us "sons" than others. A few of our fathers were in the home and with our mothers. Some of our fathers were "with" our mothers but not in "our" home. Some of our fathers weren't with our mothers at all. Some of our fathers weren't known to us. Some of our fathers weren't known to our mothers either.

In any case, we had choices for our role models. What we couldn't know or see were the models of success that didn't operate in our neighborhood. We weren't aware that our choices were limited by the circumstances of all our neighbors and the community around us.

Our community was a comfortable place.

The tree-lined streets, the moderately well kept yards were the first impression you receive upon entering our neighborhood from 25th Avenue, the main east/west vein that fed all the neighborhoods we were familiar with. Most of the homes were brick or clapboard sided bungalows with small front and even smaller back yards. Fences surrounded most of the homes with chain link, hedges or woodframes and wire of various designs. I would guess that 75% of the homes had a father and mother inside. I had a mother and a grandmother, no father, yet for some reason it never seemed to matter.

The fathers for the most part worked for the steel mills that surrounded the southern most tip of Lake Michigan. All we knew about these fathers was that they went to work and came home. Their work hours varied. One father was a truck driver, another a postal worker. We never knew what some fathers did. I never knew what my father did when I was a child. I found out in my senior year in high school that he was an excellent welder. With these examples you would suspect that all of the young

black men would aspire to these choices. I should be a welder, others should work in the steel mill or post office. In the end, very few of us chose to model our fathers or the black men in our neighborhood. We were also aware of the other side of these fathers, as well, their relationships and treatment of the women and children in their lives. Would we model this? Most of us chose to go our own way, driven by visions of what we believed we could be; beyond the world as we knew it then. As we grew in age and awareness some of us "Sons of the City" began to define our lives and our relationships by other terms. Our own terms......

As President of our Explorer Scout Post I began to strengthen my leadership skills even further. In addition to recruiting additional Explorer Scouts from our sponsoring Church and surrounding area, I began to exercise my organization and writing skills by creating a "CONSITUTION" for our Post. This document included a Preamble, Bylaws and several Acts that detailed our reason for existing and all of the ground-rules we were to operate by into the future. Exercising my artistic abilities, I proceeded to paint the backs of several aluminum chairs with the names and titles of all of our Post Officers. My Uncle Clarence informed recently that these chairs remain in the Church lower-level to this day. As I came closer to High School graduation I began to transfer knowledge, skills and responsibilities to our "up and coming" younger Explorer Scouts that had exhibited potential for leadership. Letting it all go in order to go away to school was an emotional experience for me, unlike anything I had experienced in my life.

It was like the separation anxiety experienced by lovers torn apart.

In August 1969 I left Gary, Indiana for Indiana State University in Terre Haute, Indiana. As the fourth child, I was the first to go away to College. I was not sure of when I would return.... Home.

I was not sure of ... if ...or when ... this "Son of the City" would return.

Chapter 6

Attempting Love

Attempting Love

In my early years of college, I didn't really know what love was. I never felt my definition quite matched the popular opinion on what love is. The truth was I ...."really didn't know". I hadn't seen it. I hadn't experienced it. No one had ever told me what it was or how I'd know it when I saw it. The hurt and pain of failing at love has taught me that love is allusive and that the definition changes as you and others change.

If love were to be defined for me, if I were to work to fulfill someone else's definition of love, the love I'd have would not be my own and therefore not be love at all.

Well, I compromised my definition. I convinced myself to think that I could transfer my definition onto someone else and have it become theirs. I worked at shaping my own expectations and held out that time and effort would result in this shared vision and turn it into reality. A comfortable definition of love.

The reality of this effort was disappointment after disappointment for me and my partners.

I didn't know any better. I trusted my own mind and held to my own belief that I could create my desired relationship. I had always been able to take responsibility for making my life comfortable. No one else would. Why couldn't I do that with love? Why couldn't I create my own reality? How else would I get what I needed? Surely I couldn't trust someone else to this. Trusting wasn't in my vocabulary. I certainly made no connection between trust and love.

To me, trust was emotional. Love was operational. I saw love as a matter of how I functioned and what I did for and to my partner. I didn't see any emotional side to love. Love was possessive, trust was allusive. Love should just be there, trust was unfamiliar, going or coming, giving or receiving it.

So, as I worked harder at possessing love. My partner yearned to experience and trust the feelings and the emotions that I couldn't get in touch with. My inability to give my partner the trust needed pushed them further from allowing me to feel secure in my ability to possess their love.

The cycle played out again and again, like a merry-go-round with bad music in the background. A steady revolution in constant motion, passing through the same scenes with different faces and backgrounds, ending up at the same place in the end.

My giving was in direct proportion to my receiving. My receiving was in direct proportion to my giving. A carousel that I could not get off of.

The closer they came to me, the more I needed to give. But how, what, why did they demand so much? Why couldn't they, like me, trust in themselves and be secure in that? Had I sought out people that would need me even though I was unable to supply their needs? Did I have an equal need to be needed?

Why couldn't they get their emotional security from within and just share their love with me?

On the other hand, how true was I really being to myself? Did I in fact possess this great level of trust in myself that my partners seemed not to have or had I deluded myself to think of myself in that way as a defensive mechanism?

Might I, in reality, be more focused on protecting myself, guarding my feelings, keeping "me" free from emotional harm? Was there some kind of connection between the love and security that I needed and the emotional security my partners never felt from me? In an unconscious effort to protect myself from hurt, might I have created an emotional shell around myself? Could this shell be so well entrenched that it guards me from hurt but also from the joy that can come from a relationship when partners let their guard down and surrender or open up to give and receive affection and love.

What would this require of me? Was it true that the answer to this question and my ability to act on it is key to relational happiness?

Where is the answer then?

The answer lies in the history of my fathers' experiences. By fathers, I mean that collective group of African American men that have been, since the Spanish King Carlos I, granted an "asiento de negros" in the 1500s. This European monopoly on the importation of African slaves to the Indies initiated a spiral of dysfunction in the lives of the enslaved African men, fathers and families to this day.

The ensuing centuries of despair and the spread of slavery in the west only aided in deepening the wounds and extending the recovery from emotional and relational catastrophe.

While it is difficult for most African-Americans to understand this spiral. It is impossible for most whites to even come close to understanding the damage created by slavery.

The damage was done to African-American men but equally to women. The resulting implications have born out in millions of sons and daughters over the past four centuries.

The annals of those centuries are draped in stories of families and relationships struggling to find themselves. Simultaneous stories of those few that have somehow risen beyond this emotional genocide dot the pages of time, yet go unrewarded, unrecognized, and somehow seem to drift too far away for the millions of us like them that so desperately need a re-deployment of role models and success stories throughout our society.

On one hand I must be careful and on the other hand, I must be true to my feelings when I say that the problem in African American relationships is not a male problem but equally shared between both sexes. African American men and women must come to grips with the damage done to them and own their share of the burden in its repair.

Unlearning and learning how to live and love in the 21st Century requires a new foresight and a renewed hindsight.

During this period, Brenda Manyfield came into my life in a different way than I'd experienced after riding in the car with her as she dated my best friend at the 1969 high school prom. After seeing her in the shopping mall during a College holiday break, I invited her to come to campus for our homecoming football game and a concert (The Group Tavares performed that day). She accepted my invitation. I hadn't seen Brenda since the senior prom, but I had thought of her on many occasions. We made arrangements for her visit and agreed she would stay in my apartment. I was ecstatic about the prospect.

Brenda was one of the most striking physical specimens of African-American womanhood I had ever seen. Her every move screams of strength and beauty combined as she walks. Tall and slim yet well endowed in the hips and legs; Brenda held her shoulders square and back as if to accentuate her petite yet firm silhouette. Brenda's appearance commanded respect. Her face was golden brown with wide, clear brown eyes surrounded by a full head of hair shaped in an "afro." The legs on this lady started high and went forever. Long and slender but strong and shapely, I could only imagine being in her embrace. She was the physical epitome of a dancer or an athlete.

The day she arrived on campus I had prepared dinner and was dressed to impress. As I opened the door to receive her, she was more beautiful than ever. Her smile filled up the room and made me feel great that she was here to be with me for the weekend. Dinner and the show went well. I was proud to have her by my side. The rest of the night was a brand new experience for me. After all I had done I had great expectations.

We returned to my apartment, we dressed for bed and climbed in. I rolled over toward her and we kissed passionately for several minutes. As I moved to position myself to make love to her, she pushed me back and said "go to sleep Edwin." This happened once again that night and I finally understood that she was not planning to go that far with me. Disappointed, stunned, shocked, confused and surprised, I asked her to confirm what her actions were telling me. Well, she did. She was not going to give herself to me that night.

This felt like a major setback. Something had to be wrong here. Why not? Could this be true? What had I done wrong? In the end I decided that I read her wrong. She wasn't misreading me.

I was disappointed, this was a big one that had gotten away. It felt like failure. I had failed.

My remaining years in college continued to take on a new perspective relative to women and intimacy. The once reserved young neophyte became progressively more assertive and forthright in his pursuit of pleasure. The string of affairs, relationships, loves and encounters ran the gamut. Seemingly, the less I cared, the more success I had. I selfishly bounced across campus from one to the next one, holding on to my emotions and doing only God knows what to other's emotions.

It didn't really seem to matter. Not to be misunderstood, I cared about each of them in my own way. I told them I cared. They cared too. One or two truly loved me. I couldn't truly love them. My true heart was safely locked away. Many of them wanted a long-term relationship, a few were in it, like me, for the physical love.

There was Ms. D, the freshman from, my hometown. A sweet and very petite little lady with the tiniest of features from head to toe. Her pert little lips rested on an oval face surrounded by long black hair. Her small pointed nose was perfectly placed between two almond eyes. She must have weighed all of 70 lbs. But was well shaped waist down. Her chest was small but she had a heart of gold, that was what she gave to me. I didn't want to hurt Ms. D, but I didn't love her. So we made love periodically and I ran from her for a year or so until I left town.

Ms. P was a quiet, soft-spoken parent of a child she left at home in order to continue her education. You would never have known this. On the plain or nerdy side, Ms. P was not very attractive but well built. She made it clear that she wanted me and being who I was at the time I wanted some of her too. We came together in secret on the weekends mostly and usually only for the intimate hour or so. There were no spoken expectations and there seemed to be no strings. We enjoyed the pure physical aspect of our intimacy and my conscious was always clear.

There was Ms. Deb and Ms. T from Indy, Ms. J from Terre Haute, and Ms. S from Alabama. They were completely different in every way but the "one thing" that made them all stand out was their lady-like persona. You would swear that these ladies were "southern belles" trained in the art of discretion and honor and social grace. These women understood discretion and managed our relationship in a manner befitting the noblest southern protocols. In other words nobody knew and we liked it that way.

Over the years at I.S.U. a handful of our African American student body launched a Gospel Choir labeled "The Ebony Majestics". The Choir became an excellent extra-curricular activity and social networking forum for me. Simultaneously, as we performed at Churches and Schools across Indiana and the central mid-west, the Gospel message of Jesus Christ was often woven into the various programs and agendas. In retrospect, the combination of hearing the gospel and singing gospel songs was a perfect combination of experiences to bring me to know Christ on a personal level.

Then I decided to get married. No, it wasn't just like that. But not far off.

Carol came back to school. I had changed. She didn't know. She had changed too, but I didn't know. So when she called me and stopped over, I could only think of what I had missed when she left prematurely. I had wanted her in the worse way before she left. Now I just wanted to be intimate with her. Yes, I wanted to make love to her but it wasn't the same as when I wanted to be with her before. No, I didn't tell her. I led her to believe it was the same and she ignored the truth that was before her everyday as I flirted and flaunted my newfound sexuality in front of her eyes with other women. I guess somehow that I blamed her for what I had become. Maybe somehow she also blamed herself for having to leave before we could build a relationship. In any case she was back in my life and I was bent on taking full advantage of it.

I had been fortunate to become a Residence Hall- Residence Assistant or "R.A." or floor leader as a Sophomore and after a year in that role, I became an Assistant Dormitory Director as a Junior and was given my own University paid apartment on the seventh floor of Fairbanks Hall. At the end of my Senior year I was offered the position of Placement Counselor and moved to the "Married Student Housing Unit" as a single person.

It was around this time that Carol returned to I.S.U.

I worked to let her know I wanted her and she responded in just the way I wanted. Our sex life became a sporadic reality, and my "love" never really developed. Our intimacy increased but my commitment didn't. In my mind and heart I struggled with the commitment. Something was building a degree of guilt in me.

Our first son, was born on August 5, 1975. We questioned our intentions and our visions. We challenged one another's motives and motivations and in the end decided to "do the right thing." The wedding was held in the out of doors in our Indiana hometown. Family and friends were there as we walked down the aisle and pledged our vows to one another.

The words were "...till death do we part." The truth is we were separated twice and then divorced within the span of 15 years. We had joined a Church and were active there however, I lost my willingness to be vulnerable in the relationship. I was afraid to really commit. I failed to recognize a few things. I failed to recognize that what I wanted was reliant upon what I was able to give. The fact that giving in order to receive were tied inextricably together, avoided me in return for a perceived control over my risk, and a perceived control over my vulnerability.

To be vulnerable is to risk but also to trust. Through the trust comes the intimacy and the love.

I couldn't see it then, but "control" had become my survival technique. In every aspect of my life I had learned to seek control in order to protect my self and my own interest. So, when I couldn't "control" my mate's emotional needs I got fearful. The fear encouraged me to push for more control in order to avoid the pain. Yet when I couldn't really reduce or eliminate someone else's emotional pain I just became even more fearful that the relationship would be destroyed. I was afraid that I couldn't bring her through her pain or that I'd have to give so much of myself to rescue her that I'd have nothing left for me.

I've come to find that my mate's expression of her emotion (fear, hurt, etc.) was not a plea for me to take control of anything. In fact, it's more of a request to be heard, valued and listened to. Through the listening and value expressions, she really is able to work out her own emotional issues. They say that hindsight is 20/20. In looking back, it's crystal clear to me now that my listening skills or lack of them was a major cause of breakdowns in marriage and relationships. In addition, my inability to see things from my partner's vantage-point resulted in breakdown after breakup. Taking ownership for my part in the relationship, being honest about my fears, my pain and my mistakes had avoided me.

Why was it so easy to lie to myself? Why was it so easy to be less than honest with my mate? Why was real ownership for the relationship a responsibility I avoided?

What was at the source of my fear in relationships? Then it dawned on me. Being loved was equal to being alive. If my mate was hurting or in need, my love for her means I must help erase the hurt and meet her need. If she didn't accept my remedies, she must not need me. If she doesn't need me, she doesn't love me. If I'm not being loved, then I will die.

Yes, I was afraid of dying.

Somehow my life's experiences had allowed me to equate the absence of a harmonious relationship with death. I was often times fighting for my life with partners that I loved and loved me.

Try to imagine a conversation about which restaurant to go to for dinner ending in a life and death struggle between a married couple supposedly in love. Well, it happened, ...all the time. Follow this example:

- My first wife used to complain that I was always working and never took time to take her out to dinner.

So, I call home from work one day, around 4:00 pm to tell her that I'll be coming home by 6:00 pm and would like to take her out for dinner. She says fine, with apparent joy and anticipation.

I arrive home at 6:00 pm, ready to go.

She is nowhere near ready to go. She says she's been cleaning and cooking for the children and will be ready soon.

It's now 7:30 p.m. and I'm very angry. Why? Well, it's now a life and death issue as I see it. Why? Well, she had a need (take me out, please); my mission in life is to secure her love by meeting her needs. Because she is running an hour and a half late, our reservation may be gone, my ability to please her by meeting her need is now reduced.

I'm going to fail. If I fail at pleasing her, she won't love me, If she doesn't love me, I'll die. I don't want to fail; I don't want to die, so I put the "rush on her." I pressure and push her to hurry. I tell her that it's her fault that the whole thing will be a bust. I tell her… "this is why I never take you anywhere." My goal is to have her be the blame. Again, this is a life or death issue. I don't want to die.

I'd rather see her accept the blame, the failure and own the missed opportunity for my love.

This…… instead of my having a failed "attempt at love."

Chapter 7

On Being Father

On Being A Father....

My son, Garon, came into my life and I loved him right away. He was a bubbly and beautiful baby boy with a loving personality that reached out and grabbed you. He was a happy baby with fat and bowed legs and a full head of black hair. One of our favorite father/son pass times was to wrestle around the floor and horsy-back rides. Garon helped me form my vision of father/son. I wanted to hold him and love him like my father never did with me.

I had married his mother. Garon was the product of our pre-marital relationship, but more than that, he was the product of my loins, he was, and is, **my** son. I can't lie, his existence did play a role in my decision to ask his mother to marry me. The combination of the two of them, the prospect of our being a family, the beauty of it all was what my mind's eye had always wanted. They could give me a full measure of what I believed I was ready for.

So, we three brought our lives together. Garon was my pride. I loved showing him off, taking him places and being his pal and he mine. His childlike strength and independence made him fun to watch as he grew up.

I had been working on this book off and on for the past two years or so, 1992 through 1994. On a trip to San Juan, Puerto Rico, I stopped in a bookstore to grab a magazine or something to read on the plane. As I browsed, somehow a book titled "Creating Love" by John Bradshaw captured me by it's title. I guess it was the notion behind "creating" that turned me on to the chance that I could control and manage to develop love as an outcome of a relationship. I loved making things happen and controlling outcomes so that I'm comfortable. If "Creating Love" would allow me that, I had to buy it. I didn't begin to read it until I was on my way back home.

I found the first chapter of his book impossible to put down. His reference to "soulfulness" rang familiar to my reference to "love's souls…" in my own writings.

I separated from my first wife in 1990. As a result I chose to seek marriage/divorce counsel from a psychiatrist. My sessions in his office, first alone, then with my four children, and on occasion my partners, were a challenge to my ego, my knowledge and my emotions. All three things were challenged when I heard him say… "Ed, the day your son gives you the hug your father never gave you you'll know that you're going to be alright." My emotions were challenged because I could honestly feel the warmth of that hug. My heart and my senses knew exactly what that meant. My self-esteem was buffered because I was afraid that the hug might never come. Maybe he'd hold the divorce of his mother against me. I told myself to have hope and to be patient. Being a "father" had become something different for me now as a result of the separation and divorce. More than providing economic support, I was becoming more aware of the interpersonal support my children needed and the importance it brought to me emotionally.

As the father of four fantastic children (two girls, two boys), it is painful not to be with them continually. Watching them grow over the years has been both a joy and a pain. The joy comes from all the happy times in the backyard garden or wrestling on the floor. The pain comes from the guilt and sorrow for the years I missed their presence and the years they resented my absence while I struggled to survive an unhappy marriage to their mother. Along with this is the ever-present reminder that like my father before me, I walked out on the mother of my children. Granted, unlike my father, I fathered all four children while present in the relationship and in the home. Unlike my father, I continually provided financial support for their care and participated in many of their life activities. Unlike my father, I participated in and/or supported most of their college education either directly or indirectly. So, why the pain, why the guilt?

As I search my heart, the answer lies in the feelings, the emotions. For me, nothing can replace a father's presence. That's not to say that a father's presence is the right answer to every marital dilemma. On the contrary, I'm convinced that when a father's presence is aiding in sustaining dysfunction, the dysfunction can be detrimental to a child and "father to child" relationship. However, a father can be present in the child's life even though not present in the same home with his children. I told my wife the other day…"Any woman that purposefully separates her child from his/her father (except for abuse, etc.) is creating a depth of harm to the child that she can never imagine. If she could imagine it, she wouldn't separate them, but would work to facilitate the growth of their relationship."

My experience in this area is all too real to me. Our sons and daughters need the hug of their father. They need to be able to experience love from a man in a no-strings attached, healthy, caring way. Too often our daughters are led to believe that they have to give of themselves physically to a man in order to be loved by him. I contend that the absence of a wholesome, unconditional love from their father creates this false perception of love, leaving many of our daughter's susceptible to the lies and deceit young men offer in exchange for physical pleasure without commitment. Once caught in this spiral, our daughters all too often bounce from one empty relationship to another looking for the love they never grew to know from the presence of their father. Their choices of mates are often failed from the start, because the criteria for selection were flawed, incomplete.

Our sons too, need the hug of their father. They need to be able to experience love from a man in a no-strings attached, healthy, caring way. Those of us men that missed the presence of a self-assured father that openly loved our mother and demonstrated his commitment and affection, have no foundation or example of a healthy, caring love relationship. Moreover, we have no legacy of successful relationships to pass on to our sons. Thus "the spiral" continues.

So, why the pain, why the guilt?

In part, the guilt also comes from the fear that I have perpetuated "the spiral" in my sons and their sons to come. My mind's eye envisions my sons struggling in and out of relationships with women, unaware of their own needs, unable to choose the best partner for their lives. I see them stuck in marriages founded on their own inexperience in identifying healthy, caring relationships. As a result, I'm worried and afraid. I've walked this path. I've been there and done that. In the end, there has been a lot of pain, a lot of anger and a lot of sorrow. I'd love to be able to spare them that.

Can I…?

Is this just a part of life…?

Must our children experience this as many of us have?

Or is there a way to save them, a way to spare them…?

Chapter 8

The Miracle on 25th & Jefferson Street

The Miracle on 25th and Jefferson Street

As I came back to the present, Brenda and I turned the corner onto the street I once knew as "home", Jefferson Street in Gary, Indiana. The trees were there in even grander form. The shade hung over the sidewalks and the pavement creating an envelope around the neighborhood that seemed to protect the memories we shared through the years. In contrast, the houses showed visible wear and tear, a kind of catastrophic decay that seemed to start at the gutters and cascade across the roofs and down the exterior walls of almost every home on the block. At the same time, there stood two or three homes that appeared to be frozen in time. Their structures still strong, the brick facades still neat and well maintained, somehow surviving the demise all around them.

The little red brick "bungalow" at 2575 Jefferson Street still stood, meek, soft around the edges from years of erosion, yet somehow strong and peaceful as it peeked over the row of hedges that rimmed the small front yard.

It was 2001 and the memories raced through my mind as we stood there reflecting on a joyous time, a time absent of cares or woes, a time filled with fun and games, explorations, trials, successes and failures.

It was always "home." It was always home to the brother that went to war, to the son that went away to school, to the sisters that were married with children, to those that moved away and to those that stayed. It was always "home." Now, as I stood there facing 2575, it still felt like home. Oh, how I wanted to step inside and feel the security of the four walls as they would surround me. Oh, how I wanted to return to the time when the eight of us would sit in the living room and watch The Lawrence Welk Show or hear our grandmother say "Get Ed Sullivan on there for me." Oh, the smell of a large pot of pinto beans and oven baked cornbread on a Saturday night. The savor of fried chicken, collard greens, yeast rolls and macaroni and cheese on a Sunday after church. The excitement of a neighborhood wide game of "kick the can" every summer night and cricket played with soda cans, a ball and two sticks every summer afternoon. Looking back, in retrospect, these were the images called to my mind as we stood there in front of 2575 Jefferson Street.

So we drove on, this time to 25th and Grant Street. On the way, we passed by the "corner stores" and called them by name. There was "Jerry's" and "Rucks" and "Mr. Butches" and the "garage store," each with its own set of memories both fond and frustrating. Fond memories for all the sweet sugary joy we purchased and consumed from their shelves. It had always been frustrating when we passed them by as children, without a nickel or a dime to buy our favorite candy-bar or popsicle. The memories clashed with the reality that day as we passed each corner to find each store burned out, boarded up or closed down. At the end of 27th & Jackson Street there stood our Alma Mater, "Fredrick Douglass Elementary School." The school looked relatively strong considering the demise of much of the neighborhood around it. A new painted sign replaced the original stainless steel lettering that graced the red brick auditorium exterior wall. Somehow the new sign seemed to cheapen the place. It was "spring break" so there were no children to be found and a voting booth had been stationed in the hallway to serve a local election.

It didn't feel like it used to feel. Somehow the innocence was gone.

The memories of fellow classmates sitting on the small rails all around the school, the sight of handmade fall leaves, cut-outs of pumpkins and paintings of flowers on the windows were all gone. The little boys and girls in their scouting uniforms and crossing guards with their white shoulder belts, the moms and dads standing across the street as their children crossed, were only a faded memory as we snapped a few photos to seal and preserve a piece of our past.

We drove through "downtown." The faint resemblances were barely enough to remind us of the way things used to be. The large chain stores are all gone. No more Sears, Goldblatts, Penneys, Walgreens… no more fine jewelry and specialty stores… no more dress shops, law firms or business offices. Here and there an insurance office, a state or city services office and an odds and ends store run by a new Asian immigrant and his family. Downtown Broadway used to be the center of activity.

Today it seemed to sit in a kind of twilight zone of vacant buildings between the vacant lots where buildings once stood.

For us it felt like a ghost town. Yet in my heart I knew that this town was the place my heart, body and soul was from. This place…while it stood void and stagnant in it's own "twilight" was my HOME. This place had broadened my horizons as a "young son of the city" from 1951 to 1969.

This place ….that surrounded 2575 Jefferson Street had shaped my early years. This place had brought me to Christ Temple Holiness Church as a child and was still "my Home". This place had held me and nurtured me for my first 17 years and continues to provide that sense of "HOME". This place had seen the seven of us through the bad times and the good times. Four generations lived in this house. This 2 bedroom, red brick bungalow had covered and kept us safe and secure. From this place we had seen one another grow, chronologically, physically, emotionally and spiritually. Many of us had come to know one another, friends, foes, successes and failures over the years. Each of us, over the course of our lives as brothers and sisters, had shared that strong sense of safety between these small red brick walls. That sense of safety served as the foundation and launching pad for each of us as we ventured out to become the men and women we chose to be.

This address, 2575 Jefferson Street, echoes as a kind of "song" as it reverberates in our mind's ear. These tiny walls and confined spaces never seemed to restrict our sense of reality or opportunity. This place was and is special in our hearts and minds, often begging us to return, always reminding us of a magical time….. gone by.

This place, 2575 Jefferson Street, still rings with melodies from the Kimball piano our Mother paid $300 dollars for in 1959. This piano both over stretched our Mother's meager finances and echoed familiar tunes from stagnant notes of it's brand new students to soothing sonnets and songs in their accurate and full harmony. That house overflows with life experiences we can never forget. Those experiences and memories lie underneath the long healed burn marks on my right arm. That home reminds me of my sleeping "cot", created out of an old ironing-board and two 20 gallon oil cans, jammed between "the big boy's bunk bed" and "Mom's Bed". Mom's bed had traveled up from Mississippi and survived at least one relocation once it arrived in Gary back in 1947. It served as the sleeping place for "the Girls", including Mom. So, day after day, night after night, the three girls and Mom "shared" her bed, the "boys" had their "bunk bed" and Ed had his …"cot".

Clear as day is the Muntz T.V. we tuned with a wire coat-hanger and a pair of pliers. Never can I forget the kitchen or the living room and it's function as the placeholder for our home heating evolution from the pot-bellied cast iron stove and the dark, dirty, heavy, dusty "coal" to the smelly "oil" and finally to the gas burning space heater over the years.

That house was the place we returned to every Sunday after Sunday School, Church Service, Bible Study and Choir Rehearsal. Second to our home at 2575 Jefferson Street was our "Church Home", Christ Temple.

Both addresses hold several things in common, but, my head on my Mother's lap is the fondest memory I hold common to both locations.

Grace, Guts & Glory

This address, 2575 Jefferson Street will always hold a special place in my heart as I'm sure it does for each of us. This place and her hands comforted me like a song, like a Psalm.

This place, "<u>my Hometown</u>" had given me a vision of "what I could be".

It placed a vision in my mind and a "song in my heart" throughout my developing years. My Hometown had a number of songs that had developed in me, nurtured me and motivated me for a half century.

Now, I realized that I needed "New Songs". Songs for the 21st Century.

I needed…"Psalms" for my today's and my tomorrows, …, your todays and…..your tomorrows.

Chapter 9

Psalms for the 21st Century

Psalms for the 21st Century

Psalms 2000

Her Hands

-Her hands always amazed me, somehow gentle yet well-worn over the past century, softened over the decades of nurturing and laboring at life's door.

-Her hands were always warm to the touch and warming to my face as she would caress my cheeks on the cold winter mornings in Northwest Indiana.

-Her hands were worn supple and honed like fine Corinthian leather, smooth and supple yet strong; well polished to a high gloss over fine lines and wrinkles.

-I loved her hands.

-Her hands loved me too. I could tell how much she loved me when she held my hand or when she touched me.

-Her hands transferred her message of love through my body and into the depths of my spirit every time she touched me.

-To feel her touch offered up a depth of security and a sense of belonging and comfort I have never experienced elsewhere.

-Her touch was special, above all special and different than any other I have experienced.

-To feel her touch brought warmth and a penetrating sense of connection that only she could give, a touch forged over a century, a touch shaped by a history of love and struggle, a touch born in her destiny and delivered for our destiny.

-Her hands were ever present, present to corrected and caressed.

-Her correcting hands approached my face or shoulders filled with understanding and enlightenment, designed to inform and instruct or to redirect.

-Her hands never carried hurt or harm.

-Her hands never held us back, moreover, her hands lifted us up. It was her hands that chose the direction for us all.

-Her hands signed the writ of sale.

-Her hands signed the new lease on life that freed our family from centuries of bondage and decades of disadvantage.

-Her hands chose to walk a different path, a better path for those she loved before their time.

-Her hands pressed together in prayer and lifted her body from its knees every morning and every night.

-Her hands held the words that shaped her heart and held the lamp unto her foot path as she walked.

-Her hands rejoiced at the songs sung from the faith she held in her heart. -Her hands wiped away her tears as she felt the pain from lost love and witnessed love lost.

-Her hands performed the detailed and precision work of a master craftsman at her trade yet fumbled with the gross volume of work placed on her and her alone.

-Her hands guided her through it all.

-Her hands hardly rested.

-With her hands she carved out of life a better future for herself and her offspring.

-With her hands she set the foundation of possibilities for her ancestors.

-Stone by stone, with her hand she set in motion a building process and plan that would give us the full right to the tree of life.

-With her hands she provided each of us a portion of a view of what and who we could be.

-Her hands set in place the stepping stone we could choose to launch us forward and life us up; up high enough to see over the barriers placed before us from an earlier time.

-With her hands she pointed the way, the way forward, not behind.

-Her hands held the directions.

-Her hands pointed the way, the way up, not down.

-Her hands held the directions in Word, deed and in her heart.

-With her hands she opened and read the Word and opened her heart to be read and understood.

-Her heart was clear and so was her Word. With her hands she opened to read the Words written for her heart. From her heart she shared the Word with all that would hear… from Love… in Love.

-Her hands would wipe the tears from her eyes when her love failed.

-Her hands caressed her own bosom when her heart was broken time and time again.

-Her hands would beckon … come on in… when her love would reappear, then wave "good-bye" when the night was near.

-Her hands held the ring he placed there with a vow and never failed to hold on to a hope, somehow.

-Her hands would always open the door for a true love long lost, then finally touch his urn once he had paid the final cost.

-Her hands had forgiven what she could not control and her hands would protect us from an abandoned loves toll.

-Her hands would launch us into the cruel, real world and be there to catch us if we were to fall.

-Her hands had dressed us and bathed us in front of the blazing coal stove, and her hands would cover us from the winter's cold.

-Her hands would fan us in the midst of the summer's heat and her hands never failed us when it was time to eat.

-Her hands sustained us from head to feet and always found a way to provide us a treat. From meager beginnings to moderate means, her hands were consistently present for me, present for them.

-Her hands were sometimes shaken by the losses in her life, her brother, then her mother and earlier her spouse.

-Yet her hands held firm to a higher intent, to love and care for her children... heaven sent.

-She prides herself in holding family in her hands, her children, her grandchildren, and great-grandchildren.

-Her hands tell the story of how deep her love goes and how deep it will carry only God knows.

-Her hands are trusting, kind and true, created from love for me and for you. To model and mimic as best we can, the walk of a woman that walked with her hands.

-Her hands closed the book on chapters already finished or opened new books or new chapters yet to be written.

-Her hands wrote the first words to every paragraph and turned each page for a new beginning.

-Her hands turned the pages from the book's start to its ending.

-Her hands left their imprint on the pages as she turned... symbolic of the fact that she had been there before us, indicative of her empathy for our past and our present... reflective of her depth of experience and knowledge.

-Her hands traveled roads and byways we would trod and along the way she gathered insights to our lives as they could be.

-Her hands saw our future before we would create it, before she could shape it in her hands.

-Her hands applauded the music we made, the art we created and the special marks we made.

-Her hands held our pain and caressed our fears.

-Her hands sheltered us from the cold and kept us warm.

-Her hands mixed the oatmeal and chucked the corn that sustained our bones and made us strong.

-Her hands would rock us to sleep and wake us to rise.

-Her hands had held us close as we grew and released us to do.

-Her hands would hold the hands of those we would love and embrace them as one too, as sent from above.

-Her hands would catch us when we'd fall.

-Her hands secured us all. When things went wrong or all hope was gone, her hands would help us to carry on.

-Her hands held the physical and financial support we would need.

-Her hands had earned a small wealth of resource beyond her goals.

-Her hands had toiled yet her goals were never spoiled as she refused to squander what she had earned.

-She always held her resources in open hands.

-Hands that were ever present for us all.

-Hands that never measured the big or the tall, hands that lifted even the small.

-Her hands are older now. Shaped by decades of toil, caring and love.

-Softened by charity, grace and love, her hands have run a good race on earth and above.

-Her hands are older now, but not to a fault, for her hands are ever present without a doubt.

-Her hands still sing and pray and shout as she embodies what life and love is all about.

God bless ....”Her hands” !!!

Psalms 2001
Mercy

- Grant me thy mercy…. O Lord.
- Hear my sweet songs of praise to you… in this hour hear me… O Lord
- Hear my cries.
- Grant me thy mercy…. O Lord.
- Answer my prayers
- Selah

Psalms 2002
<u>Praise</u>

- I lift my voice in honor to you… O Lord.
- Your spirit is ever present.
- Your blessings they comfort me all the days of my life.
- Bless you, O Lord
- Praise you, O Lord. God of my ancestors, guardian of our fate and our faith.
- Bless you, O Lord.

Psalms 2003
<u>One Battle</u>

- Use me, O Lord.

- The battle rages yet still with the fallen one. His purpose, his mission abounds around us and, but by our faith, in many of us.

- The battle rages

- Who is on the Lord's side?

- Who will take up his armor?

- Who will bear his sword?

- Who will bear his shield?

- The battle rages.

- I pray daily for my own strength and resolve to be a champion for you   O Lord in the face of the wicked ways of the fallen one.

- I pray O Lord, that others in the faith will gird up their loins and put on the full armor to join in the battle.

- We in our faith know that the battle is already won…

 for you would have it to be so from the beginning.

- Having been chosen by you from the beginning I wait and look forward to your will for my life in this battle.

- Use me, O Lord.

- Use me.

- What battles men wage. What strife and discontent we create in our souls and in our acts.

- What purpose do we serve? To what end do we pursue? What goal to achieve? What cause?

- There is but one battle.

- Pour out your blessings on us O Lord in these last days.

- Let our battle sound loud in all the lands. Let our victories be bright lights to those that seek your truths.

- Magnify the victories we pursue in the name of our common belief… Christ Jesus risen.
- I humble myself before you Almighty God. I ask your forgiveness for this sinner man. My prayers flow to you from my repentance and my faith in your finished work.
- Please hear my prayer, O Lord.
- Please answer my prayer, O Lord.
- Use me O Lord.
- Give me strength to stand in the midst of the battle, O Lord. Let not the sharp arrow or the sword or spear pierce my body.
- Give my arms the strength to hold up your shield of mercy.
- Give my bones the strength to draw the sharp sword of your word.
- Sharpen my mind's eye to discern the ways of thine enemies and to overcome them.

Psalms 2004
Witness

- Answer my prayers, O Lord.
- Grant me the ability, strengthen my gifts, enhance my love and charity towards all men.
- Grant me the ability to be a light and a beacon to the lost.
- Grant me the ability to be a source of encouragement to the weak of heart.
- Answer my prayer, O Lord.
- Search me, O Lord. Search my heart, O Lord.
- Forgive me, O Lord, for my sins.

- If any of my sins stand between my prayers, remove it, O Lord, through your grace and mercy.

- Let there be nothing between me and thee, O Lord.

- Hear my prayer, O Lord.

- Answer my prayer, O Lord, that I might serve you more, that through my suffering God will be glorified. That through my example God will be glorified... that through my victories God will be glorified.

- Lead me O Lord, as I witness to your greatness and power over all things in concert with the love you have given us from the beginning ... the mercy and salvation you have given us through Jesus Christ crucified.

Psalms 2005
<u>Children</u>

- I marvel at thy everlasting presence, O Lord, from my beginning unto this present day thou art always in my presence.

- The morning sun brings your warmth and glory to my face... the wind whispers your presence round about me... the evening stars shine Your grace and glory through the cloudless sky. The night silence echoes the peace You bring through our faith.

- My heart sings praise to You, O Lord, from the innocence of my childhood. In my fullness of choice I pledge my faith in Your finished work... in Christ crucified and risen.

- I pray O Lord, for your blessings upon my children. Watch over them O Lord as they traverse this earthly sojourn. Be with and in them O Lord that they might prosper in Your spirit and in Your truth.

- Be a mighty fortress round about them O My Lord,

them and their descendants.

- As my mother and grandmother stand in intercession for me O Lord, be it so that I may be a stalwart and intercessor for my children and their children's children.

- Grant them all thy mercy Lord. Pour your mercy on them as they stumble and fall. Lift them O Lord that they might return unto You mightier and armed to do your will.

- Guard them O Lord, against those that would seek to devour them, even the fallen one. Bruise his head and his heel against his evil plans. Let not even a hair on the heads of my little ones be broken by his deeds.

- I praise thee O Lord in honor and glory for your omnipotent power and your never ending love.

- Great is thy faithfulness O Lord my God.

- I rest in the comfort of your will, into your hands I rest....Your Child

Psalms 2006
<u>His Word</u>

- Precious Lord, how great thou art. How great is thy voice and how sweet its sound.

- Give me the will, O Lord, to study thy Word, to show myself approved, rightly able to divide the Word of truth.

- Use me, O Lord, as a lamp unto the eyes of others that seek Your Word.

- Help me, O Lord, to be a witness in my walk to those that don't know Your Word, to the promise that they too shall receive the word.

- Open the hearts of Christians across the world that they

might dwell in your Word daily. Send your spirit to us that we might be indwelled with thy Word.

- Help us to be steadfast in reading of your Word and meditation in the Word that we might be able to lead others and discern Your Holy will.

- We give You the honor and the glory. We praise your holy name. We fall down before you and humble ourselves in the light of your grace and mercy.

- Praise you O God, our Father, and the Word, in Christ Jesus our Lord. Blessed be the Lord for his Word endureth forever.

- In his Word we have the power to overcome the world and to become one with him and God the Father.

- One church, one body, one God, one Christ our Lord.

Psalms 2007
<u>One With The Father</u>

- How great thou art O Lord.

- How great is thy Father in heaven.

- How great is the Holy Spirit our comforter within us.

- Blessed are we that you are One in the Father, even before all the world was made, even so unto today.

- Blessed are we that we have been given you by the Father and are his and yours as you prayed the Father.

- Blessed are you O Lord, for your prayers and supplications on our behalf before the Father. How deep is your love for us O Lord, in that you saw fit and mercifully to pray our sanctification, our joy, and our protection from evil in this world.

- Thank you O Lord Jesus Christ for your intercessions on our behalf. I thank you O Lord for your prayers

and plea for me and mine.
- Bless you O Lord, my hope and my salvation.
- Bless you O Lord, my help and my protection.
- Bless you O Lord, my savior.
- Praise be to God the Father, Son and Holy Ghost.... who are One...!!!
- Amen.

Psalms 2008
Safe In Thee

- Precious Lord I seek to see the wonders of your handiwork this morning. In my zeal, maybe it's too soon, In my zeal maybe it's too cold for me in my recovery.
- All I Know is that I want to be able to hear the birds sings, see the sun rise, feel the warmth of the sun on my face.
- In your mornings shine many miracles too small and too large for man to comprehend. In those miracles is where I want to live in commune with you and with man.
- I know your doors are open. I know your entrance is free.
- Help me O Lord to be safe in thee.

Psalms 2009
Safe & Secure

- I have been safe in thee this morn. Yes O Lord, safe enough to see, safe enough to feel the bursting forward of your beauty in all that grows and becomes around me.

- Thank you O Lord, for the soft hearts that create these spaces for me, for those hearts that can see you in your beauty through them.

- Thank you O Lord, for the sight and senses to see this for myself yet while never disbelieving in you through faith sight unseen.

- I love you Lord, you heard my cry and delivered me... safe and secure.

Psalms 2010
Ore & Ore

- How you have been there, ore and ore. In my faith there you are, ore and ore.

- In my belief thou art there, ore and ore.

- Thy blessings are there, ore and ore.

- My help meet, one with me

- My battles, ore and ore, not mine but yours.

- Your power, ore and ore, is seen in each day, each moment.

- Your grace, ore and ore, there to hold me up to embrace me round-about.

- Ore and ore, you have proven that all things are possible if we only believe.

- Ore and ore.

Psalms 2011
Count It All Joy!

- God loves us. Count it all joy.

  Put God in the right spot. Count it all joy...!!!

  His "son-light" is here for us all. Count it all joy...!!!

If things aren't good , they're gonna get better with God on your side.

Count it all joy…!!!

• What a joy to cherish God's love. Count it all joy…!!!

It's like an addiction turned the right way. Count it all joy…!!!

An addictive love founded on love for life. Count it all joy…!!!

Hold tight. Let him take your heart and show you the right way.

Count it all joy…!!!

Psalms 2012
O Lord

• I'm lost without you O Lord.

You are the lamp unto my feet.

The doorway to life.

Stay with me O Lord.

You are the alpha and omega,

The beginning and the end ...

• Oh how I love Jesus.

Oh how I love thee O Lord

Your power and grace are overwhelming.

His grace and mercy brought me life and sustains me

Your grace covers me in concert with your relationship with Him.

• Your peace like a river attendeth my path.

My sorrow like sea billows rolled.

In my lot thou hast taught me to pray…..

It has been made well with my soul.

You have blessed my soul O Lord.

- My cup runneth over with joy from your grace and goodness.

  Be there for me O Lord.

  I will be present for you with honor, praise and glory.

- Thank you O God for your grace and goodness.

  Thank you for sending me the love you possess.

  That love flows through my mothers, sisters and brothers, my sons and daughters.

  Keep them all well through life and I lift them up to you....

  O Lord

Psalms 2013
Good God Almighty

- Oh Great God of Glory, hallowed be thy name...

- Thy mercy endureth forever, thy mercy endureth for all ways, thy mercy endureth a lifetime of lifetimes in spirit and in truth.

- Round about me thy mercy flows... Through and in me thy mercy flows...

- All the days of my life thy mercy wrapped itself around me. Even though I stumbled, thy mercy received me in Grace.

- Oh Great God of Glory, merciful is thy name...

- Thy grace is mine Oh Lord, thy Grace endureth forever and ever in spirit and in truth for those that believe.

- For by Grace I have been saved... round about me

thy Grace shows itself to me, yet also to the world if it could but believe.

- A great gift is thy Grace Oh Lord. A great gift is thy Grace.

- Thy Grace has followed me all the days of my life.

- My ancestors sat in your Grace Oh Lord… hallowed be thy Grace.

- I stand in your Grace Oh Lord, humble in body yet bold in spirit.

- Blessed be thy name Oh God, blessed be thy name!!!

- Thy grace hath proceeded me all the days of my life. Yet when my path led to darkness, thy Grace proceeded me and made my path bright.

- Thy Grace proceeded when the robber would bruise my heels, yet Grace gave me the power to bruise his head.

- Oh Great God of Glory, gracious is thy name!!!

- Blessed is the assurance you provide.

- Blessed is the comforter and the peace he brings in time of need. Never has your comfort forsaken me. Never has your peace alluded me in time of need.

- How great thou art Oh Lord… how great thou art!

- When in my body the battle rages, thy Spirit is mine.

- When all others forsake me, your Spirit is mine.

- Your Spirit is mine as comfort…. yesterday, today and tomorrow,.

- Blessed be a forgiving Spirit.

- Bless be our Good God Almighty!!!

- AMEN…

Psalms 2014

"From HIM to HEART to HEAD to HAND"

- As life has dealt Me it's hand, I can't help but reflect on the Man…

  … for his impact on My past, My present and My future in this Land

- My heart is full of joy and strength beyond the natural Man….

  … because I **am** from Him, to Heart to Head, to Hand.

- I ponder on **his** presence along with Me on My way…

  … And I acknowledge how I've leaned on Him from day to day.

- My mind is clear that all I have and all I can….

  … is but the result of a sequence…from Him, to Heart, to Head, to Hand.

- I know now, more than ever before…..

  … that it is Him who has opened every door.

- As life has turned from left to right and as time has turned through day and night… It has always been Him to keep Me in the fight

- My heart is full of joy and strength beyond the natural Man….

  … because I am from Him, to Heart to Head, to Hand.

- My deeds have purpose and My actions tell others of His plan….

  … that all things come …from Him to Heart, to Head,

to Hand.

- My past, My present, My future has always been in His hand….

  … it has only been Him, molding me into… this MAN.

- He has watched Me and taught Me and kept Me from the fallen Man.

- He has provided for Me when no others can.

- He protected Me and healed Me when My body couldn't stand….

  … reminding Me that everything we manifest in life comes…

- From Him, to our Hearts, to our Heads, to our Hands.

- When we reflect back on the things our Hands have done…we recognize that our choices and deeds in our Head were one.

- In truth….to ourselves, when our Hearts are in concert with God's original command…..

- Love flows and comes from….Him to Heart, to Head, to Hand.

- Love is God and God is Love, in honesty to All things above….

  … So join Me in Him, in Heart, in Our Heads and in Our Hands.

- Let all we feel and think and do, give Glory and Honor to the Man…that carried Love, from Him, to Hearts, to Heads, to Hands.

- Let us share ownership for His Hands, that held the painful nails….and His Head that suffered torture's thorns…While His Heart embraced a Love reserved….from Him and only Him…to Hearts, to Heads, to Hands.

- For OUR SALVATION comes ….
- From Him, to Our Hearts, to Our Head and to Our Hands as we daily live …. In HIM.
- AMEN, AMEN, AMEN…!!!

Psalms 2015
A Friend In Deed

- How oft a call from her or him we heed…. A Friend through life, a Friend in….deed?
- In urgency or emergency's plead…We call ourselves, a Friend in...deed.
- For financial or emotion's heed…We find a way to meet one's need…

  … a Friend for always, a Friend, indeed.
- To shelter us from cold and rain. To come to us in haste and speed…

  … a Friend forever, a Friend, in …deed.
- To be born "for us"…Our Souls to plead…
- To suffer hurt from rod and reed
- To give His Life
- To Die….and…Bleed
- Jesus…… A Friend?
- A Friend??
- My Friend???
- INDEED….!!!

Psalms 2016
A Couples Prayer

- Precious God in Heaven….We bow our heads before

you.

- We give you honor for your Grace and Mercy as we pray.
- Precious God we thank you for your Love and Blessings in our lives everyday.
- We thank you for your Son Jesus Christ our Savior and for his finished work on the Cross.
- Father God we ask that you continue to guide us as Husband and Wife…guide us as One in You, two no longer lost.
- We ask you Oh God to send your Holy Spirit to touch our hearts and minds with your Love for us two.
- We ask you Oh Lord to continue to lead us in the way that you would have us to go…as Husband and Wife….lead us as One, in you.
- We thank you Oh God for your bountiful provision for us and our Family above.
- We ask you Oh Lord to continue to provide for us in Love.
- Continue Oh God to increase our Love for one another and for our Family in heart and mind.
- Guide us Oh Lord in sharing our increase with those in need, both Family, Friend and Stranger in kind.
- Strengthen us Oh God to hear your voice and to heed your calling and the commands of Your Son.
- Strengthen us Oh Lord as Husband, Wife…… as One.
- Strengthen us Oh God in Love and Affection.
- Strengthen us Oh Lord in Prayer and Supplication.
- Strengthen us Oh God in Your Word and Meditation.
- Strengthen us Oh Lord in our Patience and Caring.

- Strengthen us Oh God as your Son and Daughter without sparing.
- Receive us Oh Lord as we humble ourselves in Your Love.
- Receive us Oh God as Yours in Heaven above….!!!
- Amen
- Amen

Psalms 2017
To Sing

- What a joy it is…to sing.
- What pleasure the melodies, to my heart it brings.
- What a gift it brings…to sing.
- A wonderful and powerful thing…to sing.
- The words in song, the rhyme in time….

  … all bring a message to hear.
- The melodies, the sounds, all music to my ear.
- Just …to sing, is the thing…I hold so dear.
- Whether happy or sad, whether mad or glad, when I sing,

  … all things fall in place.
- Whether I'm worried or sure, a song is the cure

  … that enables me to continue the race.
- To sing is the thing…that assures me.

  …the thing that releases my heart.
- To sing is the thing that secures me….

  … and fills my heart's soul…. whenever I start.
- To sing, it is a honor….

  …an honor to Christ the King.

- For he is the force behind me...

    ...and the focus of all that I sing.

- Yes, he is the source of all my singing...

    ... My Savior, Our Christ... the King.

- He is the reason why I live...

    ... the reason I have....To Sing.

- Selah, Selah

Psalms 2018
Saving Tears

- As a young boy child growing up and surviving in the streets

    I was proud of the fact that.... "I never cried".

- At those painful but frequent times that I deserved and received a spanking ..or.. whipping for doing something wrong... "I never cried".

- As I stood there or jumped to miss the sting of the leather strap or the willow's limb...."I never cried".

- I shouted with anger and pride..."You can't make me cry!!!"

    It somehow enabled me to protect my feelings. It somehow supported my sense of "honor" or my justification. In my mind, if I didn't cry...I wasn't... "bad"... I wasn't ..."wrong" ... I wasn't ..."guilty".

    I was ... "saving my tears" .....

- Today as I reflect on all those events, all of the times that I could have cried..... I have found another reason why... I never cried....

- As I have lived life and as I have wandered from that phase to this phase of my life... I have found an answer... in my tears.

- I never cried as a child… so that I might cry… as a man…

  …. I was saving my tears.
- I had been saving my tears for good reasons.
- I needed my tears to be in full supply…

  … as my life twisted and turned….

  … Toward what God would have me to be.
- My tears have become important to the cleansing of my heart….

  …. and my mind
- My tears have become warm waters that have eased my fears and relieved my decades old pain.
- My tears have become the symbol of my joys…

  …. the jewels of my soul.
- My tears are the shingles that cover my home.
- My tears are renewing like new rain.
- My tears are refreshing signs, forgiving signs….

  … not signs of guilt or blame.
- Through my tears I can see.
- Through my tears I am free… in spirit.
- Through my tears I am free… in deed.
- There is no shame in tears, nor is there blame.
- In my tears I bless "His" name.
- For it is only He that knew the days would come…

  … when I would need my tears.
- Only Jesus knew the hour and the day that my fears…

  … my tears would wash away.
- Yes, Jesus knew that the time would come when I would cry… and pray.

- Only Jesus knew the second and the minute of my pain…

  … my tears would ease that day.

- Yes, Jesus knew the time would come when I would cry and pray.

- Only Jesus knew that through my tears my sight could see…

  … the tears he shed for me.

- Yes, only Jesus knew the time would come when I would cry… and…pray.

- Only Jesus knew…"my tears"… would be shed for others,

  … as His blood was shed for me.

- His … "saving tears"… were shed on Calvary…

- As he hung on that cruel, cruel tree……

- Yes….He cried, ….He even died….

- Through His tears I now can see… that…

  …He had "saved His tears"… for me.

Psalms 2019
I Cried…Jesus Died…For You… !!!

- Last Sunday… I asked my whole Church to pray for you.

- I asked them all…to pray.

  …. To pray for your healing and full recovery.

- I asked them to pray for you as they had prayed for me.

- As they prayed…I cried.

- When I cried, I pushed back my pride.

- I had no shame … no need to hide

- I just stood at the altar and cried…..

  …. That God would move in his time…

  … and heal your body … and… heal you on the inside.

- As I cried…in my Spirit I was encouraged to realize

  … that He would bring good news.

- That it wouldn't be long before I'd see you…

  … walking in a pair of your fancy shoes.

- Last night I heard the news…

  … that my tears and my prayers were well used.

- As I see your continuing healing…

  … it's now my prayers and believing,

  … that one day soon you will be revealing

  … to family, to friends and to others…

  … the true force over all our dealing…

  … is Jesus Christ …. God's Son…

  Our Healer … and creator of your new beginning

- As you heal… and pray…

- As you…..Love and give…

- I also hope and pray for the day…that….

- … you accept what Jesus did…

- … and accept that He never hid….

- Accept the Grace and Mercy in what He did.

- Because for…. YOU…He … cried… Yes He even died…!!!

- God has blessed you….and healed you ….outside.

- Come join me at the Altar…. Where Jesus died…

- …. For YOU…!!!

- AMEN

Psalms 2020
When My sister Sings

- When my Sister sings… she gives to me…

    … a gift you cannot see.
- When she sings…. Heaven's bells ring.
- When my sister sings….

    … hurts and pains and fears

    … are only temporary things

When my sister sings.

- When my sister sings… hearts come alive

    … and Spirits arise

    … melodies and words are heard

    … that in us all our souls are stirred.
- When my sister sings…..

    … a peace resides in my bones and in my mind
- When my sister sings… Love abides

    … in the air and space where we reside.
- When my sister sings….we rest in our race

    … and in Our Savior's Grace.
- When my sister sings… her songs are so sweet

    … we feel our souls are blessed and more complete.
- In peace and LOVE, her sweet songs restore….

    … our faith, our hope, our peace, our joy.
- In LOVE she sings, in Love she brings…

    …. God's Word, God's gifts

    …. God's Grace….. galore …!!!
- When my sister sings, my heart can see…..

… the LOVE she holds for me.

- Sing…My sister….SING…!!!

Psalms 2021
Beautiful

- Beautiful….. is what she was…back then.
- Beautiful is what she is… today.
- Beautiful in what she does… for me.
- Beautiful in every way.
- Beautiful is just a word… a wonderful word to say.
- A glimpse of her, a sight to see….

   … a vision, a beautiful image, indeed..!!!
- Yes, I call her beautiful. Yes, that's not her name.
- Beautiful is as beautiful does,
- Her face, her touch, her grace…I claim.
- Oh Yes, I claimed her beautiful…
- From the start my eyes could see.
- Oh Yes, she's always been beautiful…
- Before I knew that "we" would be.
- Beautiful is as beautiful does…
- Oh, the things she does for me.
- Her touch, her smile, her hug, her kiss, my joy…
- Oh yes, a blessed joy to me.
- Oh yes, she's been my joy, my hope for all eternity.
- She stands by me to hide me… and… to let my Love run free.
- Beautiful is what she is…
- Oh so beautiful… to me…!!!

Psalms 2022
Am I My Brother's Keeper...?

- Am I my brother's keeper?
- Is my brother kept at all?
- Am I my brother's keeper?
- Who can keep him from the fall?
- Am I my brother's keeper?
- Does he see the end?
- Am I my brother's keeper?
- His salvation, only in Christ can he depend.
- Am I my brother's keeper?
- Will he be saved or lost?
- Am I my brother's keeper?
- Can he count the cost?
- Am I my brother's keeper?
- For his salvation each day I pray.
- Am I my brother's keeper?
- Our God above does say.
- I am my brother's keeper.
- My God, in you I pray.
- That to Jesus Christ our Savior,
- He will give his life this day.
- Amen

Psalms 2023
Bring Peace to My Mother

- Bring peace to my Mother...

- Oh God, to thee I pray.
- Bring peace to my Mother...
- And see her through each day.
- Bring peace to my Mother...
- For God knows her heart.
- Bring peace to my Mother...
- From the end... to every new day's start.
- Bring peace to my Mother...
- For on you alone she depends
- Bring peace to my Mother...
- Each day in prayer, on her knees she bends.
- Bring peace to my Mother...
- For what her Love and labor deserves.
- The Love and peace your Spirit brings...
- My Mother, an Angel, in your Love, preserved.
- Bring peace to my Mother...
- Let her rest assured.
- Assured that your Love always provides....
- For in your Love she has endured.
- Bring peace to my Mother.
- In Christ, Amen.

Psalms 2024
A Touch From You

- Can I get a touch from you?
- Am I asking too much?
- I am so in Love with you....
- Can I get a touch?

- Can I get a touch from you?
- Would it be too much?
- To share my Love for you,
- Beginning with a touch.
- Can I get a touch from you?
- I know you Love me too.
- It cannot be too much to ask.
- What else is there to do?
- When you Love someone so much…
- As much as I Love you…!!!
- I cherish every touch from you.
- Your touch has brought me through….
- Through the ups and downs of life,
- Your Love has been there too.
- Can I get a touch from you,
- To soothe my pain and loss?
- Can I get a touch from you?
- Your touch is worth the cost.
- The cost that comes with loving you
- It's worth the loss of life.
- My life without the Love from you,
- Was full of grief and strife.
- Can I get a touch from you?
- I trust I don't ask too much.
- I'm so in Love with you
- And I need your Loving touch.
- Can I get a touch from you?
- I pray your touch come through.

- In you I trust my life and Love
- With you Love's work is through.
- Can I get a touch from you?
- Touch me through and through.
- You touched me young and old,
- From babe in arms through fifty-two.
- Can I get a touch from you?
- Touch my mind, body, heart and soul.
- As I grow old, a touch from you,
- Will keep me safe, free and whole.
- In you.
- Amen.

Psalms 2025
Happy Birthday Lord Jesus

- Happy Birthday to you.
- Happy Birthday to you.
- Happy Birthday Lord Jesus.
- Happy Birthday to you.
- Happy Birthday for us.
- Happy Birthday for us.
- Happy Birthday Lord Jesus.
- Happy Birthday for us.
- Without your birthday we're lost.
- Without your birthday we're lost.
- Without your birthday Lord Jesus.
- Without your birthday we're lost.
- On your birthday we adore you.

- On your birthday we adore you.
- We adore you Lord Jesus.
- We adore you everyday.
- You were born to pay the cost.
- You were born to pay the cost.
- You were born to be our Savior.
- You were born to pay the cost.
- I do Love you Lord Jesus.
- I do Love you from my heart.
- I do Love you Lord Jesus
- You did Love me from the start.
- Happy birthday Lord Jesus
- Happy birthday for us.

Acknowledgements

I would like to acknowledge my Mother, Mae Frances Bliss-Hill and my Grandmother, Augusta Harris-Bliss for their love, prayers and protection that has covered me throughout my life journey. I send a special appreciation and acknowledgement to my sister Denise for her role in saving my life and giving me the marrow from her bones. My thanks to my brothers and sisters…. Mansfield, Doris, Cornell and Debbie … for their contribution to all of my life experiences growing up in Indiana and for their support to my Mother and Aunt Merline as they relocated to Houston after over 50 years in Indiana. I acknowledge my wife Brenda, my partner in all aspects of my life, my Nurse, friend and lover. To my sons and daughters, Garon, Edenn, Nicole and Marq, to my stepsons, Devin and Derek, to each of their spouses and all of our grandchildren…. Leandra, Arianna, Karielle, Derek Josiah, Jordan and John Edwin.

To my Uncles Clarence, Nathaniel and Nelson, my family and role models.

To my College Brothers, Ruben, Wyman, Charlie, Greg and Gaynell.

To Roy Harris and Scout Master Robert Bell. To Richard Bonds, Alex Moody, Eileen Wing, Warren Macaroni, Jim Wheeler, Bob McHenry, Bob LaEace, Daniel Edwin Sassi. To Jim Rose, Ernie Urquhart, Ed Kaminski, Joe Anstatt,

Larry Pickering, Paulo Costa, David Norton, Alex Gorsky, Bill Weldon, Russ Deyo, Linda Gallo, Curt Weeden, Zack Lemelle, Bob Ricciardulli, Jenny Hassell, Stan Davis, Keith Rice, Sue Sinoradzki, Sherri Salvatore, Lillian Brownworth, Brenda

Cannady, Grayce Hubbard, Steve Zollo, Linda Bryant, Linda Cavaluzzo, Diane Parks, Stephany Jones, Donna Merinsky, John Subacus, Janet Stavola, Kathy Combs, Donna and Randy David, Bruce Given, Larry Jones, Nancy Lane, Al Mays, Clarence Lockett, Frank Bolden, Ray Werts, Todd Allen, Ric Ramsey and all my associates at JOHNSON & JOHNSON, ORTHO and JANSSEN PHARMACEUTICA INC., L.E.A.D. Inc.,. and to all of my other Staff Members and associates at Indiana State University, RCA, GE and J&J over the years, and a long list of other family members, relatives, managers, co-workers, associates, Church Family and friends that have supported, influenced and advised me over the course of my life and career.

Thank you all and may God Bless you.

About the Author

Edwin Arnold Hill was born the fourth child and third son to Mae Frances Bliss-Hill and Mansfield Hill Sr. on October 27, 1951.

A 1969 graduate of Gary Roosevelt High School and a 1973 graduate from Indiana State University in Terre Haute, Indiana, Ed was the first sibling to go to College. He began his career with Indiana State University as a Resident Assistant and Assistant Dormitory Director. He moved on to the University's Placement Office as a Counselor and then moved to RCA in Indianapolis, Indiana as a member of their Human Resources staff. He advanced through various roles in Human Resources for their Records Division and Consumer Electronics business. Ed's roles included Benefits, Labor Relations, Compensation and Employment. Ed relocated to this area in 1985 as Manager, Labor Relations and Compensation with RCA Americom prior to the GE acquisition and remained with the GE American Communications Company in Princeton, NJ until 1988. He joined the Johnson & Johnson Family of Companies in 1988 as the Manager, Employee Relations and was promoted to Director, Employee Relations and Organizational Development at Ortho Pharmaceutical Inc. after three months. In 1991, Ed was appointed Executive Director, Total Quality Management responsible for developing a vision and strategy to actualize implementation of long-term quality business systems, employee involvement and long-term process improvements.

In 1993, Ed was promoted to Vice President, Human Resources and a member of the Management Board at Janssen Pharmaceutica, Inc. located in Titusville, New Jersey, another one of the growing Johnson & Johnson Family of Companies.

During Ed's tenure at Janssen, the Company won the Johnson & Johnson Sector Chairman's Award for Affirmative Action seven out of eight years, more than any other Johnson & Johnson Operating Company. The Human Resources Division had become a major partner across all aspects of the business. The Human Resources Division was a model for valuing diversity in that 43% of his staff was people of color, while 62% were female. Ed is pleased with the fact that several Johnson & Johnson and other Pharmaceutical Industry Executives have gained experience that includes tenure in the Janssen Human Resources Division. This included a General Manager for Ortho Biotech in the United Kingdom now a Vice President for another large bio-pharmaceutical company, a Vice President of Human Resources, Executive Director and two Directors in the Pharmaceutical Group, a Director in Sales Management, a Regional Sales Director for Janssen and a Director Sales Compensation in Sales.

Ed was diagnosed with Multiple Myeloma, a cancer of the bone marrow in December 1998. At that time, the majority view on treatment therapies was to undergo a process involving the cleansing and recycling of the patient's own blood along with only a minority of Cancer Centers exploring the benefit of full "bone marrow transplants" with matching siblings. Ed elected the more aggressive approach to undergo the transplant after his younger sister (Denise) matched and volunteered. The Oncology staff at Johns Hopkins in Baltimore, Maryland headed by Dr. Deborah Marcellus was found to be the most experienced and accessible facility on the East Coast and Ed underwent the "transplant" there in April 1999. Ed and his wife Brenda sold their home in Pennsylvania and relocated to Baltimore for the duration of his therapy, transplant and recuperation. While undergoing these procedures, the Hills optimistically monitored the construction of their current home on a 5 acre farm plot in Bucks County Pennsylvania.

Ed returned home and to his position as VPHR at Janssen in October 1999 and continued to launch or influence "people strategies" across the Company and the Corporation. The more significant initiatives included being the Founder and Chairman of the African American Leadership Council in 2000, the launch of the J&J INNOVATION Conference, encouraging diverse market strategies, J&J diverse talent acquisition and development, the creation of new Global HRVP roles for each of the three (3) Operating Groups in 2001, influencing the establishment of the J&J Office of Diversity in 2002 as well as its structural re-organization in 2004.

In February 2004 he was promoted to Vice President, Diversity – Pharmaceutical Group Worldwide for Johnson & Johnson and relocated to J&J Corporate Headquarters in New Brunswick, New Jersey. In this position, Ed reported to the Head of Diversity for Johnson & Johnson, a staff member and direct report to the Chairman of the corporation. In this role Ed continued to influence diverse talent acquisition and development while also supporting new team members as they assimilated into the department.

He continued to work to influence the development of "Diverse Markets Strategies" designed to accelerate the growth of J&J and in the face of 50% turnover in the Office of Diversity staff due to retirements, he drafted the organization structures and roles that exist today.

Throughout his career, Ed has been active in many different professional and civic organizations. Some of the organizations that Ed has been affiliated with are Project 2000, the Society for Human Resource Management, Human Resources Planning Society, Board of Directors for the Granville Academy, Board of Directors for the LEAD Program in Business, Board of Directors for the Trenton Boys & Girls Club, Foundation Board-Indiana State University, Mercer County African

American Chamber of Commerce and a supporter of Cancer Care, Inc. and the Multiple Myeloma Foundation.

Ed has over thirty (30) years of proactive Human Resources and Diversity management experience at Fortune 100 companies. His industry experience includes over 9 years consumer electronics and retail, over 3 years satellite communications and 18 years pharmaceutical/healthcare. He has managed staff sizes from 2 to 38 supporting from 300 to 50,000 employees in the U.S. and worldwide. He has experienced progressive advancement through all levels of HR in non-union and unionized operations. Ed is experienced at Plant level, Operating Companies and Corporate Headquarters. He has led innovative HR efforts to form overall business strategy and grow the business or reduce costs. Ed is also experienced in unique and inaugural opportunities in creating matrix organizations, appointing "out of the box" executives and performing non-traditional HR roles. He championed the cross-functional development of high potential Sales and Marketing managers through value-added experiences in the HR Division, an uncommon approach in J&J History.

Ed is valued as a contributor to developing Johnson & Johnson's launch of its first "INNOVATION STRATEGY" and J&J's current HR "Governance" approach inside its decentralized organization structure.

Ed operates on the principle of maximizing organization effectiveness through strengthening leadership and unleashing the competitive advantages resident in diverse employees in an increasingly competitive customer marketplace. He managed the HR function as partners with the business and structured HR units for "alignment" with the business. His HR Teams operated on a foundation based on solid "Policies/Practices," strong "Programs & Services," performing as "Consultants" and functioning as "Catalysts" to gain competitive advantage. Ed works to influence via one-on-one advice to the Business, HR Leaders, fellow J&J Executives and Operating Committee members, as well as through various alliances with external consulting firms, including Bench International, McKinsey & Co., Kepner-Tregoe, Drake Beam Morin,

GAP Intl. and others. Ed was responsible for HR strategy and tactics at Janssen over 11 years as the company grew from $800 million to approximately $4 billion in sales. His team installed Performance Management and Development systems that were measured and driven by the business strategy. Organization and People Excellence was one of three areas of strategic focus.

As a cancer survivor, Ed credits God and the love of Family for his life and success in his career. He has four children, two stepsons and six grandchildren. He resides in Newtown, Pennsylvania with his beautiful wife Brenda, a Registered Nurse and also a 1969 Graduate of Gary Roosevelt High School. They both are active leaders in the First Baptist Church of Langhorne, including Pulpit Search Committee, Women's and Men's Ministry Leadership, Ushering, as well as previously serving as Vice Chairman of the Trustee Board. The Hill's donated funds to the Church renovation and remodeling project in 2000 and continue to serve and evangelize in the community and beyond. Ed retired from Johnson & Johnson in 2007.

As Ed was promoted to Johnson & Johnson's Office of Diversity, the following message he received exemplifies his impact and legacy across the company:

"Congratulations on this well deserved move! Janssen is a far better company after having the benefit of your leadership, vision and heart. I know you will bring that same passion for people and "right" to the Diversity organization, which will make the J&J Diversity efforts the model for all of America. I cannot tell you how much I appreciate all that you have done for me personally. You have touched so many lives in such a positive and inspirational way and I am certainly at the top of the list. You have been a fabulous and caring leader and I know good things will continue to surround you"